3

To Donna
I'm so glad I
know you Donna.
Thank you for being
in my life.

Blessings

Olivia Sunshine

How can I keep breathing?

Losing a child, a mother's memoir.

Olivia Sunshine

BALBOA.
PRESS

A DIVISION OF HAY HOUSE

Balboa Press books may be ordered through booksellers or by contacting:

Balboa Press
A Division of Hay House
1663 Liberty Drive
Bloomington, IN 47403
www.balboapress.com
1-(877) 407-4847

Because of the dynamic nature of the Internet, any web addresses or links contained in this book may have changed since publication and may no longer be valid. The views expressed in this work are solely those of the author and do not necessarily reflect the views of the publisher, and the publisher hereby disclaims any responsibility for them.

The author of this book does not dispense medical advice or prescribe the use of any technique as a form of treatment for physical, emotional, or medical problems without the advice of a physician, either directly or indirectly. The intent of the author is only to offer information of a general nature to help you in your quest for emotional and spiritual well-being. In the event you use any of the information in this book for yourself, which is your constitutional right, the author and the publisher assume no responsibility for your actions.

Any people depicted in stock imagery provided by Thinkstock are models, and such images are being used for illustrative purposes only. Certain stock imagery © Thinkstock.

ISBN: 978-1-4525-7567-4 (sc)
ISBN: 978-1-4525-7569-8 (hc)
ISBN: 978-1-4525-7568-1 (e)

Library of Congress Control Number: 2013910357

Printed in the United States of America.

Balboa Press rev. date: 6/26/2013

Table of Contents

This book is for my four children and anyone who has ever lost a beloved child, also in loving memory of my son.

The story could be said to have been co-authored by my first born son and very favourite Angel, Benjamin.

June 11TH 1986—Sept.13TH 1991.

Acknowledgements

First and foremost my deepest gratitude goes to Spirit and the Angels for continuing to guide me even when I choose not to listen, and for their constant unconditional love. For those who have passed on to the other side, who have helped me with this book from start to finish.

Huge gratitude and love go out to my incredibly angelic co-author and favourite Angel ever, Benjamin, who was by my side each step of the way. I could not have done it without him. To my only daughter for her love and friendship as well as struggling through with me, even though she has a different path. To my three sons who have been my best teachers. I so appreciate the roles they have played in my life, giving me a reason to keep breathing.

I also appreciate the place that my best friend has taken, walking this path with me for over 20 years. She has also been an incredible support and strong shoulder to cry on.

Thanks go to my younger brother who has been a valuable sounding board for me, and a dear and loving friend. I could not have asked for a better relationship with my brother. To all my other family members and friends that did the best they could for me.

My new husband gets my gratitude; first for pursuing me in the beginning. He has been an incredible inspiration with his unstoppable belief in me that I can do anything. He is truly the wind beneath my wings. I doubt I would have come this far without his faith, trust and unconditional love for which I am so very grateful.

I am thankful for the loving acceptance and non-judgement of the people at my church. They have helped pave the road and guided me into my true way of life. To all parents that have lost a beloved child, for the common ground that we share. I bless them all with huge healing Angels.

Foreword

One of life's hardest blows is to suffer the loss of a child. A child dying is not right, it's not fair, and it just isn't supposed to happen. A child dying contradicts our instinctive belief in the order of things and the fairness of 'God' or 'Life', as well as defying our status as responsible parental caregivers. "How Can I Keep Breathing" offers insight and validation to the initial feelings and behaviours that arise from such a trauma, the struggle to keep on going, and the various ways family members cope with this kind of tragedy.

Olivia Sunshine also shows a way, through her personal experience, of turning loss and pain into an ongoing opportunity to becoming a more fully developed and integrated human being. It is the silver lining that seems so impossible to find when one's heart has been so badly shattered. This was not a quick or easy process, and Olivia did not have a formula to follow, but despite watching the negative effects the death of her five year old son was having on her husband and her daughter, she fell back on strengths she didn't even know she had to get her through this. We all have this inner strength, though we may not be aware of it, or how to access it, and we all have choices as to how we handle a crisis, and we may not be aware of that either. And we can all use some help getting through our darkest hours and worst nightmares. Olivia's hope in writing this book is to share her experience and what she has learned so that others who are going through the agony of losing a child might find some help and comfort.

The effect of losing a child resonates throughout the rest of each family member's life, even for siblings born after the death of a brother or sister. "How Can I Keep Breathing" addresses the struggle with this and the coming to terms with it. For instance, how does a parent keep the memory of a deceased child alive in a way that is healthy and balanced for themselves and everyone else in the family? A child born into a family has a lifelong relationship with that family even after death, so there are choices to be made about how to handle this, from complete silence to setting a place at the dinner table every day for the absent child, and everything in between.

Death invites examination of our beliefs about it, asking what; if anything, lies after death, and does life have any meaningful purpose? A person's beliefs have a huge impact on the reactions they have and the choices they make and beliefs are a fluid thing. They can grow stronger or change completely. When a belief is challenged, one can hang onto it for all their might, or see it as an opportunity to grow. Olivia gives a compassionate view of different ways of handling the death of a child, and shows how the spiritual path she chose helped her cope with the loss of her son, and how it changed her life for the better in more ways than she could have imagined. The second part of "How Can I Keep Breathing" is based on a mother/child relationship that transcends death, because love transcends death.

Lou Hammond of The Lost Boys Club

Introduction

In September 1991 on Friday the 13TH my whole world was turned upside down when my dear son Benjamin, five years old, was killed in an accident. Writing this book has been tremendous therapy for me, although bringing up these past memories has been difficult and heart-wrenching. This memoir book has been written by me and it is my perception of the events, which may not be the perception of others.

It is my intention to show you, the reader, through my experience how I was able to change my life for the better. Had my whole world not been turned upside down I would not have had the opportunity to see it from this perspective.

This is the journey of my personal growth over a twenty year span. My feelings, emotions and actions since my world completely changed. I have included my experience with raising three beautiful children that never got to meet their big brother and wondered if that would impact their lives or not. I also include the experience and challenges in raising my daughter, who clearly experienced the tragedy of losing her little brother and best friend.

I was directed by an angelic voice, on a beautiful sunny day in early spring of 2009 to write this book. If I did, the book would help others that had gone through a loss like this. I was also told I would be gently guided the whole way. So with this message I just had to start writing and have faith. I did a meditation and asked Benjamin if he would also guide me and be by my side through this part of my journey. This is when I was impressed with the thought he would be my co-author. Little did I know what he meant by that. Later, when I was finished writing the book, I received a message from my son that there would be a 'Part Two' to the book. He told me that he would channel through me his experiences since he left the earth plane. He told me to ask him questions, then sit quietly and write down the answers he was putting in my head.

I was also told by Spirit not to use any names in the book other than my son's first name. This I was told would help to protect anyone in my book that may not have been so forthcoming with their part, that they may feel is private and mainly to protect the privacy of my living children.

I have had a huge passion for helping others ever since I was a little girl. I have also had an incredible desire to write books. I have been writing all my life, but only for my own personal therapy. For this book I must give credit to my vivid memory.

I feel it's appropriate to give the reader a bit of my background for a better understanding of where I came from.

I was born in a big city in Canada. My mother and her mother were also born there. My father came from England in 1952 and met my mother shortly after. I have two brothers that are five and six years older than me and a brother nine years younger. I was raised in a very Catholic family and we had to go to church every Sunday whether we wanted to or not.

Through years of various therapies I was able to look back to the age of three when I was mentally given a scene of me playing and communicating with my Angels just like they were right there for everyone to see. But when I told my mother about them I was told to stop lying and never to talk like that again. I didn't understand what she meant, because they were real and I knew that, I could talk with them, even touch them and the love they had for me was definitely real; however, this statement from my mom caused me to put my Angels in the dark and there they stayed for many years until I was able to remove the blocks and allow them back into my life.

I struggled through my school years, only working on being friends with everyone, which does not give you good grades. Because of my Catholic upbringing I always felt I had done something wrong or bad. At the age of fourteen I was put on prescription drugs to calm down, at sixteen was introduced to alcohol and other drugs, not a good mixture. Then my mother passed away from cancer when I was seventeen, it was a difficult time for me. My little brother was only nine at that time. Once he turned twelve he came to live with us until he was eighteen. By the time I was twenty-five I had to go to a detoxification centre for both drugs and alcohol, but mostly my dependency on the pills. I needed to go on to a recovery program, but I was unable due to having two very young children at home. So I went home where there was little support, but a huge reason to stay clean.

In all, I learned to support myself and felt alone in that, but I made it.

I have tremendous hope that this book will help others who have lost a beautiful child and struggle to keep breathing. We are all individuals with different feelings, thoughts, and ideals, religious backgrounds and beliefs. When a tragedy hits so close to home we step on common ground together. With a heartbreaking, shake your foundation experience like this we quite often can feel that we are the only ones this has happened to, which may lead to deep feelings of aloneness and the struggles that come with that emotion.

This book is not only for parents who have lost a child, it is for anyone who has a heart and has had it broken through the passing of a loved one.

PART ONE

Mom's memoir

CHAPTER ONE

What Life Was Like Before....

It was a beautiful day in June of 1983 when my husband and I were married, in the big city where we were both raised all our lives.

He came from a family of three sisters and no brothers and I came from a family of three brothers and no sisters. Life started out pretty good although we had our ups and downs as most new couples do. Nothing unusual.

Our joy grew to an almost exploding point with the news that we were going to have our first child in six months. On a cold and snowy evening in November 1984 we welcomed a beautiful baby girl to start our little family. I was grateful that she was a girl as I grew up with all boys and definitely required more feminine energy around me.

About ten months later I said to my husband, "I think I want a boy now." Well, talk about planning, nine months later.... It was very early in the morning and we were off to the hospital. I had not gone full term so they had to do a C-section.

On June 11TH 1986 my little Benjamin was born. He was sick and only weighed 5lbs. 5oz. They had to put him in an incubator. About thirty hours later he only weighted 3lbs. That meant that he had to be moved to another hospital that could better care for my very small baby.

At the other hospital they had so many tubes and wires in him, I was very frightened. To see all the other tiny babies in there was scary as well, but I had hope, because they saved so many of those tiny infants. Then they had to shave my son's head, removing half his beautiful soft hair. Two day later when they put him on the scale he had not gained, so they tested him for pneumonia. It was positive. This whole time I had not been able to even hold him in my arms or close to my heart. I went in to be with him the next morning and caressed him through the little hand holes in the side of the incubator.

The doctor happened to come by at that time, so I asked him what was going on and would Benjamin be okay. The doctor's reply was much unexpected, he said "I'm sorry to tell you, but he is probably going to die, unless he has an incredible amount of inner strength." Then the doctor said sorry again and walked away. I was stunned and did not know what to do.

I didn't know how a 3lb. wee baby could even have inner strength. So I went back to my room, crying. I sat on my hard hospital bed and said a prayer to my mom who had passed five years earlier. I asked her if she could go into him and be his inner strength, because I could think of no other way. She must have heard me and been able to do something, because from then on he just started to get stronger and stronger. When he reached three weeks old and a little less than 5lbs., I was able to take him home and hold him. I could not wait to introduce him to his sister and his uncle, my younger brother who lived with us.

Benjamin required a different kind of care than my daughter, who was now eighteen months old and still needed a lot of attention. She really loved him though, which made me very happy, due to the stories I had been told of sibling jealousy.

Benjamin had been home just a week when my daughter was playing out in our backyard. She seemed to have wiggled her way under the fence and taken off. My brother and I ran all over the complex searching and calling for her. We continued for over an hour. I became overwhelmed with fear that someone had taken her. After another half an hour of terror I finally found her playing with a group of young children.

Oh how I hugged her so tightly while I attempted to wipe the tears from my eyes. At that moment I made a vow to myself to get out of the big city and move out to the country where I felt it would be less dangerous.

A few months later Benjamin got sick. I took him to emergency at the hospital to find that he had pneumonia again. They kept him there for a full week in an oxygen tent. Having to go home without him again was hard, but harder yet was explaining to my small daughter why I had left her baby brother in the hospital, but he would be home soon feeling much better. It felt like my heart was coming out of my chest.

Twice more in the next eighteen months he had to go back to the hospital with a week's stay each time with pneumonia. I was making an attempt at going to college to get an education, while my husband looked for work and my daughter was at daycare. This was hard on the whole family, we were so worried about losing him. What's amazing is he never got sick again after that.

Shortly after Ben turned two years old we got the opportunity to move to another province and out in the country. It was a big move with many trips, but we were all very pleased with it.

It was wonderful to wake up every morning and look out the window and see nothing, but lake and nature. One of the many reasons I wanted to leave the big city was when I woke up and looked out the window all I saw was cement.

With the help of my dad we bought a beautiful log home on 7 acres, way out in the forest. We had a huge yard and a wonderful garden for vegetables. The kids loved to play outdoors and I was grateful for the space, garden, beautiful house and spectacular view of the lake. Then we got a dog. Life was pretty darn good. Then I noticed that a new fear was coming up for me, bears and cougars.

One day I was on the porch watching the kids play. They were about to climb a tree, so I was curiously observing the differences between my girl and my boy. I felt that my daughter was thinking the whole time she was going up "How will I get back down?" I could see the look on Ben's face, he was just being, and enjoying the climb. Well he fell out of the tree and his sister scurried down just like she went up. Thank goodness Ben was okay. It was an interesting lesson for me about the differences between the two of them, very interesting indeed.

We had quite the sledding hill in the backyard which we enjoyed each winter. My brother wiped out pretty badly one day and scratched up his face. When Ben saw him he said "I want to look like that, I want to look like my uncle!" I wondered and didn't understand why someone would want to get hurt like that. My guess was that's what boys are like. Well sure as shooting the very next day Ben came in the house looking just like his uncle with a pretty scratched up face. I said "Oh are you okay my little Scarface?" He just started laughing and totally loved his new nickname.

Both Ben and I were early risers. I would get up a little before him, grab a cup of coffee and head out to the garden. Not long after he would show up in the garden with P.J.'s on and bare feet to say good morning and "I love you mom." Then off he would go to ride his bike up and down the driveway until lunch. He loved his bike better than anything.

One beautiful morning he came out with his normal message, but he didn't go running off to get on his bike. So I asked "Is something up sweetheart?"

He put his hand on his left hip, looked straight at me and said "Not really, I just wanted to tell you that Grandpa is coming today!"

"Honey, I told you Grandpa is in Australia. He went in an airplane way over the ocean." He just shook his head at me and went on about his day riding his bike till he could ride no more.

A couple of hours later I was in the kitchen washing some of the fresh veggies I had just harvested. I looked out the window that was over the sink to the driveway and saw Ben get off his bike and stand in the middle of the driveway with his arms wide open. He was facing the entrance of the driveway with a huge smile on his face. I was intrigued so I went to investigate. I opened the door and yelled out "What are you doing Benjamin?"

He just turned his beautiful little head my way and said "I'm waiting for Grandpa. I want to be the first one to give him a huge hug." Well, low and behold about one hour later and unexpectedly my dad drove up the driveway back early from his trip. I was more than a bit surprised that Ben somehow knew. Another lesson I learned that day, to really listen to the children.

In the summer of 1991 I went to the hospital to get surgery to find out why I could not get pregnant since I wanted another child.

It was a long day as the hospital was about an hour and a half away, then surgery, recovery and the trip home with many stops along the way for me to get sick from the drugs I'd been given.

The doctor told me that I was "too skinny" to have any more children! Needless to say I was not a very happy camper. I so wanted to have some more kids, they were my world. Why I accepted the doctor's diagnosis at the time, is totally beyond me now.

Before Ben learned how to ride a two-wheeler he had a tricycle and a tracker. He could not ride either of them; instead he would pick up his tricycle, put it on his shoulder and walk alongside his sister while she rode her tricycle. I found that to be very odd, but he didn't. He liked it because he could still be with his sister whom he idolized so much.

One day I went outside to call Ben in for lunch and he was nowhere to be seen. I called and called him, but got no reply. I ran back in the house to get my husband and we started the search. He was not in the yard anywhere, so my husband went up our road and I went down.

In the half hour I was looking, my fear was building rapidly. This time it wasn't someone taking him, as I had feared with my daughter years before, it was the thought of bears and cougars.

I went back up to the house to find that my husband had found him up the road quite far from the house. He was safe and sound and I was very relieved. Apparently he was going on a little hike, but not alone. He had let the dog off his leash and taken the dog with him. I had not noticed that the dog was gone. The other thing my husband mentioned was Ben had his tracker with him, up on his shoulder just like his tricycle, trucking along with the dog and not a care in the world.

Both the kids took swimming lessons at the beach. Coming from a big city I thought it was pretty awesome to get swimming lessons at the lake especially when you lived so close to it. They both passed with flying colors and earned their yellow badges.

It was a sad day for all of us when my brother decided to move out. He had been living with us since our daughter was only two months old. But he had grown up and needed to be on his own. We would all surely miss him.

About two months later we had another room mate move in. He had dirt bikes; well we had never seen Ben's eyes get so big.

One day when I was getting the kids ready to go into town Ben asked me why I only put my eye glasses on when we went into town. I was quite shy and we were still new in the community, I wore my glasses to hide myself, kind of like a mask. I had not even admitted that to myself out loud yet, but he was right. It felt that I got busted by Ben in that moment. Then he told me that I looked like a 'learner' with my glasses on. I asked him if he meant a teacher. He said "Ya, they learn people right?" I said "I guess you're right Honey."

I had a week end job cleaning cabins. My boss and I did it together and we became very close friends. I called her my surrogate mom. One day I was upset and she asked me "what is wrong? You don't seem like your old self today. Can you tell me what is going on?"

I told her that I kept getting this kind of vision. It was one of my kids being taken away from me forever. I didn't know which one or how, because I pushed it away every time it happened. It was horrifying. I said "I don't know what to do?" She stopped and came over to give me a hug and told me everything would be okay.

Ben's fifth birthday was upon us. We bought him a brand new BMX bike. He had outgrown his old two wheeler about six months earlier. At the time I asked him if he could come out on the front porch with me and invite his sister as well. So the two of them came out and I said to Ben "What do you want more than anything in the whole wide world for your birthday today?"

"Oh I want a brand new bike mom, sooo bad." He said excitedly.

"Okay then, Ben I want you to stand over here and close your eyes nice and tight, click together your heels three times and say out loud what your birthday wish is." While he was making his wish his dad hauled his new bike out of the trunk of the car.

When Ben opened his eyes and saw his bike he was ecstatic! He jumped on and drove up and down the driveway the rest of the day.

CHAPTER TWO

Friday the 13th, September 1991

I was homeschooling my kids. My daughter was in grade two and Benjamin had just started kindergarten. On Thursday September 12th during class I was helping my daughter with her math up at the kitchen table and Ben was sitting on the floor painting a picture. Looking down at him I asked "What is that a picture of Honey?"

He said "It's a mermaid mom, see?" As he pointed to the green, blue and purple, the waterline and the blond curls above the water, I knew exactly what it was.

"That does look like a mermaid Hon, keep going." Then I went back to helping my daughter with her math.

About ten minutes later I looked down at him again and the picture he had now, made me say "What the heck is that?"

He looked up at me with his beautiful big blue eyes and said without emotion "It's a dead boy, at the side of the road covered up with blood all around." I was stunned at the accuracy of the painting, because he didn't really like being in the house, or with a pencil or brush in his hand. If he was given a choice he would have been outside doing anything else.

How did he know, how could he know, where did this painting come from? Many years later I learned that Ben's painting was precognitive. That is when someone draws or paints a picture of a future event. I know he didn't know it was going to happen, but the fact is, it did. I was starting to see what a gift Ben possessed.

We had to go into town on Friday to get some groceries. On our drive back home I noticed something strange about Ben. He was just staring off into nowhere. I called his name and he didn't answer. I did it again and it took him quite a long time to come back from wherever he was and answer me. It was strange because when I looked at him he looked so far away, I could almost see through his eyes.

Still, on our trip home we drove around a sharp hairpin turn and we almost got run off the road by two logging trucks, far too close together and going way too fast for such a sharp turn. I was thankful for my husband's great driving skills so we didn't go into the ditch; it was a close call though. All we said to each other was "It must be because it's Friday the 13TH." Then we carried on our way.

The rest of the day was quite normal. I was preparing dinner and my husband had to go to the nearby city.

Most of the time after dinner I would do the clean-up and dishes. My husband and our boarder would take the kids for a dirt bike ride. On this evening my husband was not home so our boarder took the kids one at a time starting with my daughter. Benjamin came running into the house to tell me he was next in line after they got back. I told him to get his helmet on, which he did and ran outside yelling "I love you mom" and stood on the driveway in anticipation for his turn.

He had disappeared to the top of the driveway where I could not see him from the kitchen window any longer. I'm sure he didn't want his sister to get even a foot longer of a ride.

I had a friend over, we were having tea and I was making cream puffs when my daughter came flying through the kitchen door, throwing herself on the couch and said "its Ben's turn now and I might go for another ride when they get back, if they hurry."

Our dog started barking like crazy and I poked my head out the door and told him to be quiet, but he didn't stop. That was unlike him, he was a very good dog that way. Out in the country a lot of people do not have doorbells. We had a four legged one. I hollered at him again and again he did not stop. I figured maybe the bike had broken down and the guys were talking and walking up the road and that's what the dog heard. They did not show up.

Now I was starting to get a little concerned because it was quickly getting dark, the sun was going down. With the dog still barking and my stomach starting to turn, my daughter said with her arms tightly across her chest, "They better hurry; I want to go for another ride before it gets too dark out. Ben's having a way longer ride then I got!"

A few minutes later someone drove up the driveway. It was another friend of mine. When she came in I asked her if she wanted a cup of tea.

She said "No, you have to come with me, there has been an accident." So I put my shoes and jacket on and climbed in her van and asked her "Is Benjamin okay?" She did not answer me, but the look on her face horrified me. "Please tell me he's okay, please, please, please!" She just stayed silent.

Being brought up a devout catholic, I was praying and praying the whole way. We got up the road and I saw police lights going, thinking to myself "I hadn't heard any sirens." That could have been why the dog was barking so much though.

We were directed to the side of the road and put in a police car. We seemed to sit there for ages. Finally my friend turned to me and said "Olivia, Benjamin is gone, he has passed away."

I'm not sure I heard her right! Then I realized that this was no joke nor would she pull such a thing on me. I bolted from the police car where I was met by a police officer right away. He didn't seem to want to tell me anything. I asked him "What has happened to my son?"

He looked all around then said "I have to find my supervisor Ma'am."

"Oh no you don't, you will just tell me right fucking now!!" I yelled

"I want to know what happened right now! Is my son dead?"

Then he looked at me and said "I am sorry to say, but yes he is."

I felt my heart break, shatter on the spot and my stomach came up to my throat. I took as deep a breath as I could muster and asked again in a very quiet voice "Could you please tell me what happened?"

I remembered that the police officer could not look at me. As he stared at the ground he said "They went down a logging road and it had a chain across it." I was horrified! I put my hand up to my throat and looked up at the officer.

He said "No Ma'am, the chain did not hit there. It hit the bike tire which stopped the bike right away and your son was squished between the bike gas tank and the man with him. Then the bike flew backward and they were both thrown off. This may not help you right now, but your son was killed instantly." Well, he was right. It did not help at the time, but it did later on.

"DARK, TOO DARK, I CAN'T SEE HIM! I CAN'T SEE MY BOY!" I shouted, "I need to see my boy!" I heard someone say that I should not look, which made me angry.

So I asked someone to shine a light on him for me. Thank goodness my request was heard and a flashlight was shone on my boy. All I could really do was to kneel down on the road and kiss him goodbye. They didn't want me to do that, but I did it anyway, because I needed to.

I stood up and then screamed at the top of my lungs. I must have moved the mountain. I was in total shock, shaken to my very foundation, my heart hurt like I had never felt before.

I remember an ambulance attendant coming up to hug me, saying "You have to cry."

I replied in a daze, "I can't." What I heard next would have shocked me had I not already been there.

She said "If you don't cry I may have to pinch you." She should have known that some people in shock can't cry immediately.

My friend drove me home, but home was never the same again. Now I had to tell my other friend, but worse than that, my daughter. I had to tell my daughter that her little brother, classmate and very best friend would never be coming home again. "How do I do that?" I thought to myself. She is only six and a half years old. So, I told her, but was not sure that she understood. But right then I did not know what else to do.

Just then the phone rang and it was my husband. "Hi, I just wanted to tell you that I am going on to the next town and I'll be a couple more hours."

"NO, you have to come home right now. Something has happened and you need to come home right now!" I yelled then hung up the phone.

About fifteen minutes later I was sitting outside on the porch wrapped in a blanket, still not crying. I'm just staring into space not believing what had happened or knowing if I could even breathe. My husband drove up the driveway at that point, got out of the car and said "What happened did my Grandmother pass?"

"No, it wasn't your grandmother, it was Benjamin." I could not even look at him. He did not believe me, which I could understand. He got mad, thinking I was messing with him.

By then I was having huge problems breathing. It felt like I was choking and grasping for my next breath like it wasn't natural and I got very hot although it was a bit chilly outside.

"It's true," I said "They went out on the bike after dinner, down that logging road you guys always go down. This time there was a chain across that road and the bike hit it."

He punched the log wall of the house. I thought he had broken his hand. "I have to see him. I have to see him right now! I won't believe it until I see him myself!" He shouted. I went into the house and phoned the funeral home and told the fellow that we had to come right away. He said that it was pretty late, but decided he would let us in. It was late, it was about 1:30 am, but time meant nothing to us.

The town was thirty minutes away but it seemed like we made it there in fifteen or even less. Everything was surreal. We did not speak, but I repeated over and over in my head that this could not be true and I would wake up at any moment. I don't know what was going through my husband's mind.

There we were, looking at our beautiful five year old son, bruised and lifeless, just his body. He was gone. Everything was silent and all I felt was pure emptiness.

We were, living every parent's worst nightmare. Neither of us had any concept of time. Our whole world had stopped dead in its tracks; we were not even sure what to do or how to keep breathing.

We did not want to leave the funeral home, but we had to go. We drove home without a word to each other. What could we say?

When we arrived home, my friend that stayed to watch our daughter said she had finally got her to sleep. She hugged us both and left.

No sleep for me. I did not want to close my eyes. I didn't go to bed, but just sat on the couch, not wanting sleep, I was actually amazed that I was still breathing.

I didn't want to be alive. It hurt far too much. What was I going to do tomorrow and the next day and all the days to follow without my boy? I didn't know if my husband slept that night. I really didn't care. I just wanted to be with Benjamin.

I experienced emotions and feelings I had never had before. One of the things I felt was an extraordinary pain in my abdomen. As Ben was a C-section, it felt like someone had just stuck their hand in my tummy and ripped my baby away from me. The physical and mental pain was awful and unbearable to say the least.

The next day I had to make the phone calls to tell the people that I loved and held dear to me that my son was killed. That is when the tears started and didn't stop for months and months. When it came to my younger brother it was so hard, I really don't remember, it was all a blur to me. I do recall how difficult it was to get those words out, "Benjamin was killed in an accident last night...."

We went back to the funeral home to make arrangements for Benjamin's funeral on Monday afternoon. While we were gone from the house a friend of mine called to see what time she was supposed to come over with her three kids for their play date. Of course it had slipped my mind. My daughter answered the phone and said "You can't come over anymore because Benjamin died last night."

My friend bawled her out and told her never to say anything like that again. Then she said "Let me talk to your mom or dad please."

My daughter said that we were at the funeral home but that she could talk to her uncle. My brother, who had driven for hours to be by our side, gave her the bad news.

Friends and neighbours dropped by with flowers, cards and food (Who could even eat?) I look back now and that's what people do and it was very kind, but I just wanted to be with Ben.

At the funeral home I could not stop crying which made it hard to speak. They were very kind to us and asked me to pick out some songs Ben liked. Also they wanted me to write a little something about him. The songs were not a problem, but I could not write anything. Every time I thought of something, like he was so beautiful I would stop myself and say "OH MY GOD, HE IS GONE!' I can't do this."

I did not want to go back home. I just wanted to die and still could not figure out how I was breathing. I think if you asked any parent the day after their child died, "Do you want to go with them or stay and live through the hell?" Most would want to go with their child or would trade places with them in a heartbeat. Once we got home, family and friends began to arrive, some from afar. I didn't even care. They were all well-meaning, but I was hurting too much for a visit. The whole situation and the people seemed surreal and it seemed like I was in a constant fog.

On Monday, the day of the funeral, my brother drove our car with my husband, daughter and myself to town. We still had no concept of time or anything else for that matter.

When we got to the funeral home my husband said that there was no way he could go in and he was just going to sit in the car by himself and I said "Okay." What else was I to do? Then my daughter said that she could not go in and ran outside plopping herself on the ground under a tree. So I asked my brother if he could sit with her outside so she wasn't alone. Realizing that I was going to be all by myself up front, I didn't know what to do. I needed someone to hold me up, I could hardly even walk. "HELP ME SOMEONE PLEASE!" I yelled in my head.

Finally my brother, God bless him, talked my daughter into coming inside. The three of us sat up front and I don't remember a thing after that.

I couldn't say it was a "good" funeral or a "bad" one. It was for my five year old son and something felt very wrong in my head and my heart. I really didn't even know how many people where there, because I never looked. The only person I did notice was our boarder who no longer lived with us.

After the funeral, we put Ben's casket in our car, a Toyota station wagon. Again my brother drove. I could not drive and it was quite obvious that my husband couldn't either. We went straight to the little church in our village. At the grave yard it was me, my brother, husband and daughter. Only one other person was there, the fellow that was the graveyard keeper. We had not wanted anyone else there. It was an extremely hard time for us all.

The kids went to Sunday school at the little church sometimes. Ben absolutely loved to ring the church bell. He always wanted to climb up the rope and stay there. I was surprised he was the only one out of all the children wanting to do that.

The graveyard keeper unlocked the door of the church for us so my daughter could go in and ring the bell in her brother's honour. Every time I hear a church bell now it reminds me of that day. It's funny how such a beautiful sound can have such a different effect on you when you've been through something like that, or change any situation to a different perspective.

My husband who had a drug addiction previous to the accident was really high on this day, (to numb the pain I suppose). He was filling up the hole so fast, too fast. It looked to me like he was going to have a heart attack. To be truthful at the time I didn't even care. The whole time we were at the graveyard I was being held up by my brother, otherwise I would have been lying on the ground, due to having no strength left at all.

I could not even stand up. No wonder I didn't know how I could still be breathing. I actually did care about my husband and could not have taken it had he had a heart attack, but I didn't have the strength to worry. Now didn't seem to be an appropriate time to talk to him about my concerns with his drug use. The devastation of losing a child was too overwhelming for me to get anything else in my head.

Back at the house just up the street, people were filing in with more food, cards and flowers. The looks on their faces showed that they didn't know what to say, but their tears expressed how they were feeling. Everyone that had come through the door that day had wet eyes, young, old, big and small. It was so hard for everyone. That's when you think of the innocence of a child then you ask "WHY?"

Right away my husband locked himself in the bedroom, my daughter ran outside and I was left to talk to all those people that I knew had good intentions, but....

The next day everyone's lives went back to normal. I didn't get that. How could my whole world just come crashing down and everyone else just go on like nothing happened? That is when the anger first started to surface.

Time crept by so very slowly.

I was having a hard time with my daughter. I didn't know how to talk to her, what to tell her or even how to be a mother anymore. She needed me so badly, but I could not be there emotionally. I was so lost. Her dad was either not home or locked in the bedroom. I somehow felt I didn't have the right to be a mother anymore.

I was so upset about my daughter and I was talking to someone who suggested that I get her into some grief counselling. I was grateful for that and phoned the school. I couldn't teach her at home anymore and didn't want her to be alone so I put her back in the school system. The counsellor took her on right away. I never thought for a moment that I should, or even could get counselling for myself.

I seemed to be going downhill. I could not sleep or eat. Everything I put in my mouth felt like it was going to come back. Every time I closed my eyes I saw the accident. Sleep was nearly impossible.

I decided to go see the doctor, because I had lost so much weight. I had gone from about 110 pounds to 92 pounds. Being a former pill popper in my late teens and early twenties I did not want pills, but I desperately needed sleep and some suggestions as to what I could do to help myself.

The doctor gave me eight sleeping pills and then warned me, "If you don't get eating and gain some weight I am going to put you in hospital." That scared me enough to start eating small meals. The pills helped me get some sleep, but best of all, there were no dreams. I was terrified to dream.

My friend, who had picked me up the night of Benjamin's death, came for a visit one afternoon. She said she had something she wanted to tell me. I told her "Go ahead as long as it is not going to make me cry more." She told me that she had had a vision of a huge pair of hands, God's hands, with Benjamin sitting in them. He was swinging back and forth with a big, warm smile on his face. He was safe and happy she said. This made me feel good and a bit better.

Later that night when I went to bed I was crying and wondering why would Benjamin not come to his mother? I believed my friend with all my heart, but was sad it was not me. Years later I found out that I simply was not ready, at that time my pain was blocking any visions of love or peace.

Time continued to tick away, slowly. My husband began taking more and more drugs to numb his feelings. My daughter was doing her best at being an only child. And me? Well, I felt absolutely alone and lost. Most people stopped calling and coming over by now and I felt unsupported and alone in my grief.

I went to a friend's house on Thursday nights. We had what we called "The Stitch & Bitch Group". They were all very supportive, but none of them had ever lost a child. The ladies taught me how to crochet and I began crocheting about eighteen hours a day, it kept my mind busy counting all the stitches. I started with rag rugs then moved on to teddy bears of all sizes and with all kinds of materials. I did this for a long time. I even developed my own pattern and called them 'Benjamin Bears.' But I could not stop crying.

Four months later we had our first Christmas without Ben. Our daughter was now seven years old. She woke us up early all excited. We had a hard time that morning because we did not want to go through this day. We sat there watching her under the tree ripping open her presents, trying so hard to feel some kind of excitement for her. All we did was cry. "It just is not fair!" was all we could say to each other. I found it so hard that I was not even able to notice our daughter's reaction to her parents' mood, and not being able to do anything about it anyway.

I suggested we go to my older brother's house to get away. We could have dinner there, then turn around and come home. Everyone agreed, so we set out for the five hour drive.

We had dinner, a little visit and then left. It was too hard. My brother had a family with two kids and a wife and everybody was having a great time. Somehow it felt wrong to us, the uncomfortable feelings were strong and I did not want to show that to my brother's family, on Christmas day, that was not fair to them. I am glad we went through, if nothing else for the ten hours of driving, which was better than staying home. I'm not even sure if we went on the long drive for my husband and me or for my daughter to be with her cousins.

It was a huge struggle to try to be happy when inside I only wanted to die. Birthdays, and holidays were the worst. At the time I was not the type to care about what others thought of me, but now I wondered. Should I still be crying? Should I have stopped crying by now? Should I be feeling so unattached from my husband and my daughter? Should I be making an effort to get my husband off the drugs? And where would the energy come from to do all of that? And how the hell did God think I could handle all of this, all by myself? You know the old saying "God will not give you anything you can't handle!" I had many questions, ones I wanted and needed answers to. Who was going to answer them?

CHAPTER THREE

Life goes on, just keep breathing....

Our dog was an outside dog. Just after Christmas we let him in for a little visit and he knew he had to stay on the kitchen floor, not on the carpet in the living room.

The entrance way into our living room from the kitchen was a log arch. Ben use to sit in one of the corners and he did "Armstrong push-ups" there, (amazing young man he was). Armstrong push-ups are when you do a handstand, leaning against a wall and then do push-ups, while you are upside down. Our dog put only his head on the carpet and started sniffing the corner. I didn't pay much attention to him. The next time I looked over, he had his nose snuggled right in Ben's corner and had real tears coming from his eyes. I had no idea that an animal could cry! I know they have feelings, but to shed tears? I did not know that. I told my husband to look and we both had a good cry ourselves.

Five weeks before Ben passed away we had sold our house. The people that bought it thought it would be a good idea to pay us out just after Ben passed. This was not a good time for us as we were still in shock. However I know their intentions were good.

They were very kind people and said we could rent the house for as long as we wanted. It was an investment for them and not a home they would be moving into.

We previously had a plan for the money, but the plan kind of died with our son. We had planned to buy a piece of land, live in a trailer and build our own home, then in time start a family business. As for the emotional state we were in the money definitely got spent in the wrong way.

A friend sent a book. It was called 'When Good-Bye Is Forever. Learning To Live Again After The Loss Of A Child', by John Bramblett. I immediately read this book. It shed much needed light on our situation for me in many ways. I believe the reason that this book helped me so much was because at that time I felt we were the only ones in the world this happened to. The story was well written by the father of a two year old that was run over by a garbage truck. His older children and wife wrote of their experience in the book as well.

The book quoted frightening statistics. In 1990 seventy-five percent of parents divorced after the death of a child. I did not want to be one of them.

Later on I believe I understood why they did this. People change when something like this happens to them. We were most certainly changing. But at this early stage we were unaware of this in ourselves, let alone each other.

There was another book I received called 'December's song'. It was written by a woman who had six children. Five of them had passed away in five different situations. I read that in the first couple of pages then put it down; it clearly was too much for me to swallow then and even now. I wondered how I could keep breathing and could not imagine what that woman had gone through.

One day I went to a doctor's appointment with my friend as I was her pregnancy coach. I had been sweating so much as I sat on the floor at home making Benjamin Bears for hours on end, that it started to concern me. So I took the opportunity to ask her doctor if he knew why I was sweating so much. He said to me that he figured it was my body's way of still crying, that if it wasn't coming out of my eyes it was still going to come out somehow.

My friend's doctor also gave me a book, which I thought was a very odd one to give to someone who had just lost a child. It was about a husband and wife midwife team. I cannot recall the title. There was one story in the whole book that really interested me, about a lady who had given birth to twins, a boy and a girl. Both of the babies were very small, but the boy was smaller than the girl and not doing very well.

The lady was informed that the little boy was not going to make it. I believe the lady had a Spiritual background. She held her baby close to her and said to the little fellow, "I love you very much and it's okay if you have to go, but could you please come back to me when you can stay longer?" Then she kissed him on his little forehead and told him to go to the Light.

About ten months later that lady had another baby and it was a boy. When the boy was eighteen months old he was put down beside his three year old sister and they were very close to the same size, due to the girl being a twin and the boy being a healthy single birth. I felt something move in me when I read that.

As I was not raised in that belief system, reincarnation was a new concept for me. I immediately wanted to check this out and anything about life after death.

I have an investigative personality and had many questions as to what really happened when my son passed. Some of my questions were "Where is he now? Had anyone met him, helped him over and if so whom? What happened, what process did he go through?"

My heart was broken and I found more and more that I was questioning the faith and belief system I was raised in. My old religion taught that if someone was not baptised, they would not be welcomed by God, but instead would stay in a limbo type place or purgatory as some called it. That had never made any sense to me. I did not feel that a loving God, (I always felt in my heart that God was a loving God, not 'The Judge') would leave an innocent child in a place like that. What would be the purpose?

That took me back to the night at the funeral home and looking at my beautiful son's lifeless body and wondering how a loving God could consider anything but taking this innocent soul into his loving arms. That was my turning point when it came to my belief system and the time when it began to change.

At the time, since I was such a loner on what I was going through, I didn't know who to ask the questions that were burning in me. So I took it upon myself to do some research. At the time I did not want to talk to other parents who had lost their children, and I couldn't talk to any of my friends because they did not know what I was going through. Any religious clergy was out of the question for me, due to my anger with God, the God that I was taught about when I was younger. Nor was I able to talk to my husband as it seemed we were worlds apart. So I started this journey on my own and read a multitude of books on those subjects.

One night I was so angry that Ben was gone; I opened my bedroom window that faced out to the forest and yelled at the top of my lungs, "How could you leave me Benjamin? I didn't even get a kiss good bye!" I then closed the window and crawled into bed. With tears of anger and sadness streaming down my face, I tossed and turned and in what seemed like a couple of hours I must have drifted off.

I had what I thought was a dream that night. Ben came to me. There was the most brilliant light I had ever seen. It seemed to be overwhelmingly warm, bright and loving. He came closer to me and the light was so bright I could not even see my surroundings only his beautiful face. There were no words spoken, but it was somehow put in my head what he had to say. I was told that he was fine and happy and that I would be too. Also that he would always love me very much. Then I took his little head into both of my hands and kissed him all over his lovely face. I woke up with his teddy bear clenched in my arms and a different, unfamiliar feeling in my heart.

The following morning my neighbour came over with his three year old daughter. I said I would watch her that afternoon. We sat and had coffee and before he left I decided to tell him, since he had an open mind, of my dream. The first thing he said to me was, "How do you know it was a dream and not real?"

I had no idea that it could have been real or what "Real" even was. He said it sounded like Benjamin paid me a real visit. I had to sit with that one for a while.

My religious upbringing told me it could have only been a dream and there was nothing else to consider. This was the time, I believe, I started to open up my mind, little by little. I was also questioning the faith in which I was brought up in again.

I now started to get a bit excited at the thought of a true visit from my son. Like the one my friend had, when Ben came to her. She said hers was a vision not a dream, because she was fully awake.

A couple of hours later my three year old friend and I had a tea party. We were sitting at the kitchen table and she seemed to be looking just past me to the right. She suddenly said "Olivia, you don't have to be sad about Ben, because he is standing right beside you, I can see him. He did not really go away and he says he is doing great."

She was so sure about her message. I was amazed, a little excited and unsure, because I didn't see or feel him there, but for some reason I completely trusted her message. When I was young I could see, feel and sense things, but was told it was wrong and not to do it again. I didn't remember it at the time, but I do now. What a shame to put a wet blanket on a young soul's precious gift. I now know those gifts should be encouraged and those children listened to.

So I started playing the "What if" game. What if my husband had not gone out the night of the accident? What if it was just a nightmare? What if he was really just lost and would walk through the door at any moment? That has got to be the hardest game on one's emotions. I do not play it anymore, as I realize the game is part of denial.

I was having a difficult time without Ben. We had notches in the log walls showing how much both kids had grown in the time we lived in our log home. Every time I passed by them I broke down. I wanted to move and gave notice without talking it over with my husband.

We could not find a place to rent, so we put everything into storage and the three of us moved into our twelve foot travel trailer. We had to find a pet sitter for our dog and our cat and that was difficult. The excitement of camping-out lasted a whole of two minutes for me, but my daughter held her excitement much longer, thank goodness.

I also experienced my first Mother's day without Ben. It was awful and I cried all day. I did not feel like a whole mother and certainly not worthy of a celebration. I did try hard for my daughter who had lovingly spent the better half of her day making a beautiful card for me. It still was incredibly hard. I also was wondering if I had made the right choice to leave our home, because we were still in the little trailer and not able to find a place to rent.

The next month was Benjamin's sixth birthday. I felt sick, sad and incomplete. The day seemed to last an entire week. I was not sure that I was going to get through days like this, because again I felt like I did not want to be here. At those times the pain was much too hard to bear. Surprisingly, I was able to keep breathing.

We finally found a house to rent after three long months of camping then sold our travel trailer. I never wanted to see it or go camping again.

We tried to settle in and get our daughter ready to go back to school. The house was a dump and quite run down, but better than the trailer. At least it had a lot more room. We all welcomed back our belongings from storage and the dog; unfortunately our cat did not make it back to us. It was still so hard to be anywhere without Ben. We were slowly adjusting, but each of us at different rates. Even our dog was having a hard time; Ben and he were great buddies.

Our daughter went back to school, but because we lived so far away she had to get the school bus down at the corner. It was not a long walk and didn't warrant driving her there or picking her up unless we were going somewhere after.

On the first Friday of school in September we had to go to town so we drove down to the bus stop to pick our daughter up. She was not there and we did not pass her on the way. We waited and waited but no bus. I told my husband that we should start driving to the school, what else could we do?

I was terrified that every corner we took we would see the bus in the ditch. I am not normally a worrywart, but once you have gone through what we did it most definitely changes your thinking patterns when something is amiss. Right now I was experiencing for the first time flashbacks of Ben's accident. I now wonder if my husband was experiencing the same because we did not say a word to each other as the tension built stronger each corner we turned.

We finally pulled up at the school without seeing the bus. It had been fifteen minutes, but seemed more like a day. I ran into the school, scared half to death. As I walked into the office there was my daughter. I ran up to her and enveloped her in my arms; just then her teacher came out of a room where she was trying to call us to say our daughter missed the bus. I said that it was okay. She knew that it was close to Ben's first anniversary and said "No it's not okay." I lost it and cried the rest of the day. However she was right it was not okay. It was a truly horrible experience.

That week-end was the first anniversary of our son's passing and it was hard on all of us. My husband and his friend were walking around our yard when they heard a small sound coming out from under an old piece of plywood. They picked it up to find a tiny kitten about two weeks old.

A couple of days before that a bear and her two cubs had been hanging around eating apples from the tree above the plywood. We figured that the bears must have eaten the other kittens and the mom. The pregnant cat was left behind by the previous renter. My daughter and I even took pictures of the bears. The cubs were so cute when we were safe in the house.

We all welcomed this little kitten, and viewing it as a special gift from Benjamin. That was in 1992 and I still have her in 2012; she is over nineteen years old.

The three of us had our second Christmas in that house without Ben. Nothing seemed to be getting any better. I still found it hard to celebrate anything, especially when I could have been experiencing joy at least for our daughter. I did wonder if joy would ever come back into our lives or if it had died with Ben forever.

For a gift for my daughter and her dad I decided to put together a collage picture of Ben. It was in one of those family frames with ten to twelve pictures. Going through the photos was so hard that I found myself resorting to an old habit. I drank a small bottle of rum. That was so not good. I cried and cried, but learned a lesson and it will not ever happen again. I believe that booze and/or drugs blocks healing and I didn't want to do that, as I had a drinking problem in my late teens, early twenties along with the pill addiction. Needless to say we had another sad Christmas.

Shortly after this, we moved again into what we thought was going to be a much better home. We were about thirty kilometres away from our last place which meant I would have to drive my daughter to school and pick her up every day. We just kept plugging away at life and I tried to enjoy my alone time on the long drives to and from the school.

CHAPTER FOUR

It still goes on, life that is....

My husband's drug habit worsened, because of this he had a hard time finding work. Sometimes he would go out and not come home for two days. Most times I was scared that he would not come home at all. What could I tell my daughter? How would I explain to her about her dad's physical absence and his emotional absence when he was home?

I knew why he was doing drugs, but could not do anything about it. It was not something we could just sit down and talk about, due to his secretive life style. What made me so upset was that I didn't think he could start healing when he continued to block the healing with drugs all the time. He just did not seem to care about himself or us anymore. We did have huge problems with communication, but we continued to try to have our marriage work for our small family. There were even times when we all went for a walk or watched a funny movie together and enjoyed it as much as we could.

I spent most of my time reading and cleaning to keep busy and keep my mind off specific things. I was also struggling to keep our family together no matter what. This was not an easy task when it came to my husband or my daughter for that matter. I found it hard just dealing with my own feelings and emotions. I felt it would be easier for me to just run off on my own, but I could not bring myself to do that nor did I want to, deep down inside.

When I was seventeen years old my mother passed away. I didn't know at the time that I had a choice, but looking back now I realize I did have options. The choice I made was to look after our big home, my dad, my little brother who was nine at the time and go to school. I also had a job, a boyfriend, and a bit of a social life. I found it very difficult to cope with it all. That is when alcohol abuse entered my life and stayed with me much longer then I desired. Thank goodness that is all in the past.

One day I went to see a lady who did muscle testing. That is a way of asking your body questions about your health, emotions, and even Spiritual things. I found it fascinating because I believe my body knows what's best for me and therefore cannot give an incorrect answer. I had a question that I wanted her to ask my body. I asked "Why have I not been able to get pregnant over the last six years?" I did have surgery in the summer of 1991 to answer that question, but the answer I got then was so vague it didn't make a lot of sense to me. I didn't really know what she was doing, she was kind of moving my legs back and forth to get answers as I lay on her massage table.

After a few minutes she opened up her eyes and said "I cannot tell you why you have not been able to get pregnant, your body can only tell you why you are not pregnant right now. You have a rather large cyst in your left fallopian tube. You have put it there or manifested it there emotionally because really you do not want to have another baby for fear it will be taken away also. If you do want to have another baby you can

35

get surgery, but the cyst will probably come back. I suggest you get rid of it the same way you put it there."

Well to be honest I had to sit with that one for a little bit. She said I could do some meditation, have some alone time and talk to God, Spirit or whomever I saw that higher power to be. If I really did want another baby and was not afraid, this technique would most likely work. She felt I would get pregnant in about a year and she saw a boy.

I went home feeling more encouraged then I had in a long time. First of all I spent time releasing some anger and fears, by writing, burning what I wrote and then letting it go. This process took me about a week, every opportunity I had to work on it I would go into my office and write. Then I had to think and feel if a baby is what I wanted and I did that process while having some long hot baths. It was a good way to learn how to relax, meditate and just be, it also felt pretty good.

I was given the opportunity to take a reflexology certification course. I decided to take the offer and enjoyed the course and the knowledge I obtained. Reflexology is a form of alternative healing. It is applying pressure to certain points on the feet, hands and ears that coincide with organs in your body to clear away blocks. I worked at it for about six months before I discovered that I really was not that passionate about it. Another opportunity came up to learn massage and unfortunately the same thing happened, I loved the knowledge, but I lacked the passion to do either as a career.

You see passion was so important to me; I did not want to do anything without it. I had learned that for me, when I do something with passion there is very little work involved, because I love to do it. At this same time I also discovered that a lot of my passion may be buried six feet under, as they say.

Apparently I was not yet ready to bring the passion back. Part of me just wanted to get back to life, but the other part was still grieving and didn't know if it was okay to move on. I really didn't have a clue, because I had not been here before. I didn't know if there was some sort of rules to the whole grieving process. I was feeling torn and was wondering "Was it okay with Benjamin for me to move on?"

I was diverted from those thoughts by another move we made and wondered if that is one of the reasons we moved so much. Every time I felt like moving on emotionally I put it aside to move physically, each time maybe learning just a little bit more.

I could no longer hide my husband's drug problem from our daughter. She asked so many questions, due to her inquisitive personality and his behaviour. To be honest I told her that he was that way because of what happened to her brother. I wasn't trying to blame it on Ben's accident as much as trying to excuse her dad's behaviour. What was I to do or say?

I buried myself in more books, meditation and started doing writing therapy. My writing therapy was basically writing down my thoughts normal, but sometimes strange, then I would usually burn the evidence so no one would ever find it. I always felt that if I wrote something down I was able to get it out so it didn't build up in me. In some cases seeing it in print helped me as well. I believe, looking back at it now, that it was helpful in releasing some of the anxiety that I was going through. Had I not done it and kept it inside I think I would have burst at some time. I am sure that without my writing therapy it could have been ugly.

It wasn't just Ben's absence in my life. I was still feeling badly about not giving my daughter the attention I thought she needed. I was also dealing with my husband's stuff by hiding it from others and still trying to do all the things a normal wife and mother does.

Here we go again, another move after less than eight months. I guess I may have gotten bored if I wasn't so busy packing and unpacking, searching for another place to live then more packing and unpacking. I was starting to realize that every move we made I had packed up all the emotional baggage each time and taken it with us. Then it dawned on me that we were not running away from anything, just running into more stuff.

It had now been just over three years. I was still lost, still struggling and still sad. I wasn't crying as much anymore, but I did find out that something like this can catch you off guard and bite you in the butt very hard and without warning. I know this from driving to my friend's house, which I do a lot, and I have to pass the accident site, most times its okay, but sometimes I can't stop the crying for hours. I suppose the energy of sadness at the site is still strong.

We did not have a phone and lived way out in the bush this time. When my husband took off in our only vehicle for a day or two, I only had my daughter, who now was nearly ten years old. I felt guilty sharing too many of my woes and adult issues with her at her young age, but really what else could I do? I couldn't write all the time and I didn't have anyone else I could talk to.

I still did not feel worthy of getting any kind of help for myself from anyone, plus I never knew when my husband would be home with the car. I could not fix what happened in the past. I found out after trying endlessly that I could not fix my husband either. I felt so alone, yet continued to try and keep our family together.

I had the opportunity to have a long talk with him about his drug problem and how it was affecting the rest of the family. He seemed remorseful and wanted to get some help. I suggested detoxification as I had experienced that many years ago myself and it worked for me. He said he really did not want to go, but he would do it for us. I was a bit hesitant knowing one must do that kind of thing for themselves if they really want help.

I made arrangements and drove the hour and a half to take him to the detoxification centre. I drove home alone with so much hope that he could now start healing, and then we could start healing as a family. Also I wanted my real husband back.

Two days later I went to a friend's house for a much needed visit and some companionship. When I arrived home a couple of hours later, there he was on the front step. He said detox wasn't for him and that was the end of that.

Back in 1988, just before Ben's second birthday I made the decision to go to a detoxification centre to clean myself up. I felt if I was a better mother, wife and feeling good on the inside that everyone around me would be better as well, but I had to start with me. I went for my dependency on pills and alcohol and stayed in the facility for ten days. I could not go to a recovery centre as I was needed at home, so I had to do my recovery on my own. I found that I had little support from my family and friends, but I plugged away for my two babies and myself. I never had another pill after that, but I continued to struggle with alcohol for a while longer until one day I stopped that completely also. It was an important part of my journey.

Again my husband and I tried to work things out. I listened to what was hurting him and he listened to me. In that conversation it felt that maybe we would win this battle after all. He was going to clean up and I would stop my nagging at him to provide him the space he needed and I continued to support him in any way I could.

CHAPTER FIVE

Finally, some wonderful news....

Early on in 1994 I started getting sick every morning. I knew I was pregnant, but could hardly believe it. All I had in my head was the surgery in 1991 when the doctor said I couldn't have any more children. I had totally forgotten about the lady I had gone to see one year earlier, however I had not forgotten to do what she suggested.

I finally made my way to the doctor, had the test and yes, I truly was going to have another baby. I was so ecstatic that it was hard for me to even drive home. I was actually in shock, overjoyed and felt a sense of peace. We had been trying for over eight years. I was so grateful to get another chance. Every time I touched my belly I felt the joy and hope of new life and it made me cry tears of joy.

Our daughter was also excited and that was wonderful to see, because she had been so very sad struggling though her process of grieving and being an only child. She was going to be ten years old once the baby came and a wonderful age to both help and enjoy the baby.

I believe my husband was terrified. If only we could talk to each other, honestly and from our hearts. While I had worked with my meditating, forgiveness and letting go of the fear, he unfortunately had not. He was concerned with how we would be able to look after this child and open our hearts.

We tried to talk, but when he said he was happy I found that hard to believe. He just did not have a happy expression on his face nor were his actions those of a happy person. He just seemed scared. I thought perhaps he was feeling he would now have to let go of the memory of Ben. I did not know how to tell him that he could always remember Ben, keep in his heart, and welcome a new baby into our lives at the same time.

I had a healthy pregnancy physically. Mentally a lot of things were going on in my head and many questions like "Would I be able to open my heart again? Would my daughter and husband be able to open up and except this new life?" One of the biggest questions for me was "Will this fill the hole in my heart and the hurt in my whole being?"

Emotionally I was stressed mainly about my husband. Since the news of my pregnancy he seemed to be more upset, not caring if he lived or died. That was hard on me, but as per usual we kept plugging away and ignoring important issues that would come up and bite us later on.

My due date was December 26TH. I did yoga and meditated all the way through. I also enjoyed my pregnancy immensely.

Two days before Christmas my husband attempted suicide. He tried to overdose. I was afraid to take him to the hospital to be honest and he wouldn't have let me. I knew having this baby was affecting him on a much different and deeper level then he was sharing with me. I had to keep my chin up for my daughter and the baby due in three days. I had to pull us through, no matter what it took.

Inside though, I was a total wreck. I was worried about my husband so much and the effect all of this could have on our daughter, the baby and me. How was I going to get through it all and, I hate to say it, "Keep Breathing?" I was terrified on the inside for all of us. But as I complained about my husband not sharing his true feelings, here I was hiding mine. I knew the truth though.

We struggled through another Christmas. My husband was a bit out of it, but he managed to hold it together for our daughter. My dad and little brother came for the day and that was wonderful to have the break from everything else. On the morning of the 26th I took down the tree and put away all the Christmas decorations to get ready for the baby.

On December 27TH, two days after Christmas our son was born. He was beautiful, healthy and a good weight. My heart did open as I looked at him and I wondered how I could have even been worried about such a thing. Honestly there was still a small part of me wondering "Did it open all the way though?" I'm not sure if it was all the way, but I was truly grateful.

It was a fantastic birth, my daughter on my right hand side supporting me with a cool cloth and my husband on my left holding both of my hands. The amazing part was for the first time I truly felt both my mom's and Benjamin's loving presence. I'm not sure if I was delirious at the time although I had not had any drugs whatsoever, but I swear I saw Spirits in the room with us. As I look back now, I believe that there were more Spirits in that room than humans.

We got home the next day with our new beautiful baby boy and began, what I thought would be our new life.

Again another "Runaway" move. This time it was a new area five hours away. I had two brothers, their families and my dad there and was hoping for some family support. My little brother had always been a great support for me as well as my dad. I found out later that I really needed more than what was there.

Each time we decided to move it was to run away from the problems my husband and his lifestyle had caused in that area. Although some times the home was not a healthy place, with things like bad water and faulty structures. We had to take what we could get and afford at the time.

Being in a new place was difficult. I didn't have my dear friends, just my brother and dad. My older brother was very well known in this town and we look alike, so it seemed most people knew me, but I did not know them.

I also noticed how much I was still living in my story "Oh woe is me, I lost my son." If anyone asked me how many children I had I would have to go into 'MY STORY." I didn't like that anymore. I decided to start work on changing it. That meant more books and research not to mention going within and meditating. I continued being worried about my husband and his behaviour.

My husband was having a hard time finding work and when he did, we were so behind financially it was difficult to make ends meet. Not to mention my daughter was having a hard time being accepted at her new school. I found this town to be quite 'Clicky' if you know what I mean. At least I had this beautiful baby boy to keep me going. He was a wonderful diversion. I look back now and see just what a saviour he was for me.

As time went on, things didn't get better. The fighting between my husband and I was not good for anyone in our home. I suspected that he was having trouble with the fact that it seemed to him that I might be getting a bit better. What he did not get is, I was still hurting and hurting very much. I guess you could say, that I was moving on in what I thought was a better direction for all of us while he was still covering everything up with drugs.

So my daughter, the baby and I moved out, to an even smaller town another half hour away, but the smaller the town the "Clickier" it got. My poor little girl sure did have her share of struggles. There was one good thing; the separation relieved a huge amount of pressure in our home. That was wonderful for the three of us. We were even able to handle short visits with my husband without fighting. I wanted to believe he was doing better without having to worry about us and he knew he was welcome to come and see that we were doing well.

Our son needed some minor dental surgery. The hospital that did this surgery was a six hour drive away. My dad came with my son and I for support and I promised him I would take him to see his best friend in that area as well. My husband stayed at my place to look after our daughter so it all worked out for everyone.

The surgery went well and we spent an extra day down there for fun and to make sure there were no complications with my boy. After surgery the three of us had a good time visiting my dad's friend and then a great drive home. My son slept the whole way, which was great for him.

Upon our arrival home I had a wonderful opportunity to talk and listen to my husband about where he was at, in all of this. He finally admitted that he could not seem to get it together. He was still so angry about Ben's passing and just didn't think he could make it.

Then he told me that he figured out that he or we had done something so wrong that God took our son from our family to punish us. He said Benjamin was six feet under and that was the end of the story. He had not one ounce of hope left in him. My heart sank for him and all of us.

We cried together, he was crying because of what he believed to be the reason that Ben passed away, I was crying because I thought that was so sad. I still wondered how I could keep breathing, but now I understood his relationship with drugs. He didn't think he could keep breathing any other way. I was so sad for him, but I could not change his mind or what was in his heart. I didn't want him driving to his place like that so I asked him to stay the night.

Perhaps I had more faith. I was positive that I felt Benjamin sometimes and I knew in my heart that I would be with him again when I passed. I also had come to believe that it truly was Ben's time. This is what kept me going, I had to believe, I just had to. At this time I was also reminded of Ben's pre-cognitive painting of the dead little boy and what all of that meant.

I had to be strong for my daughter and new son. I also knew I had to be strong for myself. I was still very angry about the loss of Ben and what had become of our family; it was a kind of hell on earth that is for sure. I continued to pray, meditate and read. It must have been helping because I was still breathing and able to bring back my mothering skills that I thought I had lost for good.

My husband came home and we thought we would try again. This did not last very long. The yelling and screaming started up in no time. It wasn't just him. I could bellow pretty loud myself. I knew it was doing something because my daughter was always taking her little brother in his stroller to get away from us. I was glad they were getting along, but at what expense? We could not keep this up any longer so he moved out.

I found out shortly after he left, that he had left something behind....

CHAPTER SIX

Some more wonderful news....

What my husband had left behind was another baby. I of course was overjoyed as was my daughter. My husband was terrified at another child coming into our lives. How was he going to support all five of us when he could not even manage four.

I was lonely where we were. I just could not find any friends and felt that the whole area lacked in support for us. With my daughter still struggling in school and out of school I decided, it was time to move. I so desired to be back with my friends, as did my daughter. So I planned the move back to what I called home.

I invited my dad to move in with us and he was excited about that. My dad was on medication for a slight mental imbalance, so he was a bit of a handful at times, but the love and support I received from him completely outweighed that. He packed up his small room where he was staying and waited patiently for me to do the same.

It took me a while to get my whole place packed up, so for a little bit of a break we all climbed in my car and made the drive to look for a place to rent back "Home". We got lucky and found a very nice place.

My husband did not help with the move as he said it was my decision and not his. He did come to visit though. There honestly was less stress in our home when he was not living with us.

It was a hard move for me due to being pregnant, but we all survived. I felt a hundred percent better being around my friends for loving support and having my dad with us.

Again I let my husband back, in hopes that I could get some kind of help with the baby coming soon. In the beginning he was such a great dad that I was hoping to see that same fellow surface, but I felt that part of him may have gone with Ben.

Ben's fifth anniversary had recently passed. I took some time to myself and went up to the accident site. I talked to Ben and told him how much I missed him. I also did some forgiving and letting go. Later I discovered things like this have to be continuous.

Mid-November 1996 we had another boy much different than the last time, but I was truly grateful to have my husband by my side. This little boy came a bit early, and weighed only four and a half pounds just like his big brother Ben. We had to go to another hospital that was better equipped to look after this tiny soul. Through the grace of God and a very special Angel on the other side he recovered quickly. Thank you God and thank you Benjamin!! Believe me we were in no mental condition to go through anything other than quick recovery.

I found I could only give so much of myself as it did take an extra effort to look after this tiny, little baby. I had to send my dad back to my brothers and of course we planned another move. I know now that this one had been a mistake, but there were lessons we would not have obtained anywhere else. My husband, three children and I moved back to where we started, not in the big city, but in a small town near the big city where we were both raised, out on the prairies.

We still seemed to be having hard times with just about everything in our lives, mostly our marriage and it made me wonder if we should have brought these two boys into such a lifestyle. They were so good for me though. My husband did get a job, but had troubles with money when he got a paycheque. My daughter, now age twelve, was acting up a lot, getting into her share of trouble. I most certainly had my hands full.

Another saving grace was we had chickens that kept the boys and I busy. It was peaceful where we lived, but something was missing, something very important to me.

I wondered if it was Ben or that we were so far from where we buried him. I so wanted to go home, even though this place had been my home for most of my life. The kid's grandparents were not too far away, just in the big city and they enjoyed spending time with the kids, plus the fresh eggs of course.

I must admit I've lost track of all these moves. I was not able to last more than a year and a half when I stated "I have to go home!" This time we were not running and it was my decision, so we packed up again and moved back to the lake, where the boys were born and where my Ben was buried. "Home Sweet Home!"

It didn't seem to be any better except for my friends, my support system. My husband's drug habit became unbearable. Now I was lost and did not know what to do. I tried talking to my husband about getting some help again, but he said it was too hard. His heart was broken and drugs helped him forget that. At this point I had given up and as dumb as it sounds I wondered if it would help me too? Very bad, bad move on my part as I got hooked, in no time. One thing I did learn was that it did not help me forget. It made everything much worse.

Well, my parenting skills went downhill, I thought we were struggling before, I had no idea. It was one thing to have my husband on drugs all the time, but with me there as well we had no one of sound mind looking after the children except our daughter now thirteen, had been strapped with that responsibility. A couple of months later I took a much needed and very scary, deep look into the mirror and what I saw completely frightened me. I knew this was not what I wanted or what my kids deserved and it sure was not what Ben wanted. I made a choice at that very moment to stop the drugs right away and if my husband didn't want to that was too bad, but someone had to raise these beautiful children, accept the incredible gift that was bestowed on us and I wanted it to be me.

I prayed to Ben for his help and asked if he could round up some more Angels as well. I then had a long, hard talk with my husband and said that we had to get it together, we had been very blessed with these boys and our daughter and it was high time we both started living again and accepting our responsibly as parents!

He said he would try harder. The cleaning up process required another move, as where we were living was not a safe environment for our family, but it was the only place we could find to get us back to the lake area. We did stay around the lake this time.

CHAPTER SEVEN

Even more wonderful news....

I was so full of hope. My husband was doing pretty well. He got a new job that was away from home and that was fine with me, because it wasn't as stressful around the house. I was "squeaky clean" now and really enjoyed raising our three kids. Even my daughter was making better choices. I believe that she needed to be here at the lake too. It was almost like the lake and mountain area was a healing environment for us.

Shortly after the last move I was informed that again I was going to have another baby. This time I have to admit I was pretty surprised. I sent a birthday card with the news of number five on its way to my husband where he was working and did not hear from him for two weeks. Again this kind of news was too hard, but it wasn't something I could keep from him.

He chose to cave in and fall off the wagon again. I was beginning to think there was no way to get him to stop doing drugs. He also lost his job.

I decided to just work on myself and to be the best mom I could be. He moved back with us and looked for other work. I must say it was hard on me emotionally, but I had a huge reason to keep it together and I did my best.

In March 2001 we brought another boy into our lives. I could not stop thinking what a wonderful gift we had been given, three boys after our tragic loss. We had a beautiful family to look at as long as you didn't look too closely.

Two weeks after the baby was born my husband felt compelled to move back to the big city to get work. I said that would be fine, but I had to stand my ground, "No more moving the kids!" So the kids and I stayed and I put all my time into raising them with as much love as I could possibly give. It was going pretty well.

Raising four kids on my own was not so bad, but finding time for me was. The oldest boy was now in school so he would walk to the bus stop with his big sister every morning. I was able to get lots done with only the two youngest at home, but still had little time to me.

When the baby was about six months old I got a phone call from my husband with some bad news. He had been arrested and sentenced to one year in jail. Now I was really on my own, but for some reason I felt that I had been given a gift of time, time for my kids and myself.

It was then that I chose to make time for myself, rather than just wait for it to happen. I decided to wake up at 4:00 am every morning including weekends. That gave me three hours before the children were up. Sometimes the baby would awaken and need me, but I usually got him back to sleep with a little tender loving care. I started self-help books and workbooks and kept a steady pace for over ten months. I appreciated the time so much and I found out things about myself that amazed me, upset me, surprised me, and made me quite sad, but it was all good and I felt awesome having the opportunity to do this work.

I also began going to a meditation group that I enjoyed immensely. One evening we had a guest at the group, a physic medium. She looked at me and said "You have lost a son to the other side, have you not?" I replied "Yes", with widened and moist eyes. I was astonished that she knew. "He is with you a lot and wants you to know how much he loves you." She paused for a moment to allow me to wipe my eyes then continued. "He tells me to let you know that you need to keep going forward, that you are doing a great job and have wonderful things in your future if you stay on this enlightened path." This time I listened and totally believed. That was such an encouraging message. I felt uplifted and that feeling stayed with me a long time.

A short time later, my daughter felt she needed to get out on her own, to spread her wings. She felt compelled to venture back to the big city where she was born. I had to let her go; though my heart ached and I was terrified. I asked her to call me all the time, but she did not call enough. I suppose she was a grown up at the age of seventeen. She thought so anyways.

Now, it was just me and my three sons and a whole lot easier. I was still getting up early. I chose this time once a week to correspond with my husband who was now clean. In our letters we talked about all kinds of things mostly the boys' development and the comedy they brought into my life. We also wrote about our opportunity for a fresh start when he returned from jail.

The boys' and I developed some wonderful rituals and habits. One day a week we had 'Craft Night' after dinner, we picked a different craft each week unless it was a big project. I was truly amazed at how creative they were. One day a week was dedicated to one of us, 'Mom's Day' or one of the boys, where we had to be extra kind to them and maybe make them a card or something special. Every night at dinner we did our 'Highs & Lows', going around the table telling what our high of the day was and our low. Then we would go around again and say three things we were thankful for that day. Lastly we all made a wish for ourselves then a family wish. This was an enjoyable practice. Even the boys liked it and we've kept it up all these years. We did have to make some changes, not doing the low anymore, but replacing it with one thing we love about ourselves and then about our family. My oldest boy suggested we stop the lows, because he felt they were too negative.

When the baby was eighteen months old my husband returned. He was clean and found a job right away. He joined us in our evening rituals and was found to be rather crafty himself. It was all well and good, except I felt that he did not have that sparkle in his eyes that attracted me to him so many years ago. Really I had not seen it since that tragic day of September 13TH 1991.

Great joy! Our daughter came home about a month after her dad and even got a job at the same place with him. It was incredible to have our whole family of six at the dinner table doing our high points, gratitude and wishes every night, I was in my glory.

Unfortunately my bliss did not last long. Maybe I should not have built my hopes up so much. My husband was staying off drugs, which was great, but he started drinking more than he usually did and so did our daughter. I found that the boys and I were spending a lot of time outside on walks and going to the park. When we were in the house I spent a lot of time reading to them in their bedroom. Normally this would be good, but it felt like we were hiding out. It reminded me of when my daughter felt she had to take her baby brother on walks all the time for them to get away from all the ugly stuff coming from their parents. How the tables had turned. We just kept this up and plugged away at it all.

On Benjamin's birthdays I would make as many cupcakes as Ben's age and we would all sing happy birthday. I tried to keep his memory alive and well. Even though the boys had never met their big brother, they thought very highly of him. We talked about all the neat and funny things that Ben had done. I felt this was very healthy and healing to the three of us. I had developed a little quirk or habit, every time I ran a bubble bath for the boys or myself I would write Benjamin with the bubble bath. When I did the dishes I would just write Ben, with the dish soap. I still do that.

Around a year after my daughter and husband returned, they had both been drinking and had a huge blow up. They said a lot of harsh and hurtful things to each other. She took off slamming the door loudly behind her. I tried to talk to her dad, but he was far too angry, so I went out to search for her, only to find her just as mad.

The next day when I was working and she was babysitting her brothers for me, she packed up all her stuff. When I got home she said she was going to see an old boyfriend and would be back in time to watch the boys for me the next day. After I put the boys to bed I needed to have a stress relieving hot shower. While I was in there I had a strong feeling that she was not going to come back, so I cut my shower short to go have a look in her bedroom. Much to my horror there was nothing in there. She had completely cleaned it out everything and I hadn't even noticed.

For the next two and a half months I had no idea where she was, and lived in fear for her safety. I had a hard time not knowing if she was okay. Apparently she did call a couple of times, but her dad answered each time, so she hung up.

The whole time that she was missing I felt like I had gone back to that hell I was in when Ben first passed away. I was scared to death for her and the not knowing was killing me. Another unfortunate thing was the whole episode made my husband slip off the wagon and go back to drugs. His bad behaviour returned almost instantly. I had come so far with my inner work and the boys and I had done so well in that year and a half alone. I had decided that I could not, nor would not go through this again. I spoke to my husband and told him that it was not working out. I was exhausted, and the boys were too important to me to risk any harm coming to them or myself. I had to ask him to leave and to leave for good this time. He pleaded with me for us to go to counselling, but I was far beyond that. He refused to leave our home.

When he left the house to go out the next day, I grabbed a few things, the boys and we left. I had a dear friend that let the four of us stay with her for a week. I went to family court and got full custody of the kids and then let my husband know what was going on. It was then that he finally decided to go, and he went back to the big city.

The boys and I returned home and started packing for our next move. I felt it was going to be a fresh start for us. I was feeling some anxiety for the boys, thinking that they would miss their dad. They say that everything happens for a reason and maybe the year and a half the boys and I spent together was getting us ready for our next venture. I wasn't sure, but I was going to use that experience to encourage myself that I could

57

pull this off. I was having a bit of an issue with not being able to keep our family together, but I thought this was best for all of us.

A few days before we left I was doing some last minute packing and the phone rang. "Hi mom, it's me."

My heart sank and at the same time I was overjoyed to hear her voice. She was alive, safe and sound. I told her what had transpired and that her dad was gone. She was the one feeling overjoyed now. One of the things she said to me when she and her dad were fighting was "I am going to do something about him, because you never will!" Needless to say, she was glad of my decision. We finished our conversation with lots of loving words and her promise to come and see us soon.

The third night in our new place, after the boys were all tucked in bed I took some time to lie down and have a meditation. It was bizarre. I saw my husband and I sitting on a huge beach and behind each of us was a pile of luggage. His pile was much larger than mine. I was trying to teach him that if he was able to fully forgive, the luggage would disappear and not be so heavy or such a burden. He tried it and a few of his bags did disappear. Then our daughter showed up with her own pile. Then almost all the bags in her dad's pile reappeared. All of a sudden we see this incredibly handsome young man walking towards us. He was wearing a t-shirt with a blazer, suit pants rolled up to his knees and bare feet. As he got closer I realized that it was Ben. He looked right at me, motioned for me to come with him and I responded in a heartbeat. We started walking away down the warm beach. He was handsome, strong and emulating incredible loving light. I looked deeply into his gorgeous eyes and asked, "What about your dad and sister, do we just leave them there?"

He said "They have too much luggage; they will learn to forgive in their own time mom. You have to allow them to walk the path they have chosen, just like you have. Have faith in them mom, I do." Then he disappeared into the mist and I came out of my meditation. WOW, I had to ponder that one. I must say it was a fantastic and moving meditation or was it my imagination???

CHAPTER EIGHT

Just me and my three boys....

We were getting our lives organized in this new place. The boys were now nine, seven and two and a half. This was where my life really began to change. I did a tremendous amount of cleansing. All the stuff I had not used in years and had just been moving from place to place was now gone. It went to the thrift store, the dump or I enjoyed burning it in the several ritual bonfires I had at that time. It felt absolutely fantastic and I truly gained a sense of freedom from this liberating act.

Benjamin's seventeenth birthday came. Sometimes his birthday would go by very well, and sometimes it was so hard. I found it most difficult on special birthdays like sixteenth, eighteenth, or twenty first, but his seventeenth was very hard for me and I could not understand why. I went to a friend's house and we were talking about the trouble I was having with this one as opposed to his sixteenth, which I believe is a very special birthday. Then just as I was leaving she asked "What happened to you when you were seventeen years old?" At first I didn't think that would have anything to do with Ben's seventeenth birthday, but it was about me and how I was feeling. When I was seventeen my life took a big change when my mother passed away. My friend explained how we not only hold certain events from our past, but certain ages can trigger those feelings and emotions as well. I started thinking that must be why I noticed the whole time my daughter was seventeen I felt a little strange. Now I understood and this concept made some sense to me and was worth my investigation, as it came to the forefront again a couple of times.

About six months after Ben's passing I was sent a video tape that the mother of a friend of mine took. She was from Texas and really liked my log house so she taped the house and the children playing. Her grandchildren and my two kids were practising for the Christmas concert at our community hall and she was not going to be there for it, so she taped the rehearsal they had. When I received the tape I was home alone and decided to watch it. I tell you it is one thing to look at memories in pictures, but when they move, talk and are so full of life it is quite a different thing. I cried for what seemed hours. I hid the video away and didn't tell anyone.

One day the boys and I were driving home from town when I distinctly heard Ben's voice say to me, "Show my brothers the video you have of me, mom." I was surprised at hearing him. When we got home I fished it out of its hiding spot in my hope chest and asked the boys if they would be interested in taking a look at it. They all said "Yes."

The part of the tape with all the kids playing in our yard was only about three or four minutes long. I put it on and found myself studying the boys' faces for their reactions. The youngest was not yet three and was not all that interested, but the middle one's face was completely lit up. The older one who seemed to be the most interested watched intently then said to me, "Why did you bleach his hair when he was only five years old mom?"

I laughed and said "I didn't bleach his hair, he was a natural blond. Out of all five of you he was the only one to get your dad's blond hair."

For the longest time I had been praying and wishing to have a dream of what Ben would look like grown up. I longed to see him at about seventeen years old. In the mediation I had when we first moved into that house, he was about eighteen and ever so handsome, but I still wondered if that wasn't my imagination?

Shortly after his twelfth anniversary I had that dream. In the dream I was in the kitchen doing the dishes. My husband was standing there talking to me, and all three boys were playing nicely and quietly in the living room (this is how I knew I was dreaming). All of a sudden our daughter comes running in the house yelling "Mom, dad you are not going to believe this. Ben didn't die! I found him, he is just outside, come, come and see for yourselves."

I said "How could you do that, how could you say something like that to us and hurt us both so much?"

"Oh but it's true. Come and see he is waiting outside for you both!" Her dad followed her but I could not move. I was like a stone. I could hear that he had been let into the house and his dad was saying how much he had missed him. Then my husband introduced him to his three little brothers. Meanwhile I was able to move enough to take a little peak around the corner at him and boy it sure looked like it was Ben.

"Mom, are you coming to see me?" Ben said. Something pushed me out of the kitchen then I had to go over there. My heart was pounding so loudly it's a wonder it didn't wake me. I went up to him with shaking hands and sweating palms and he grabbed me and hugged me tightly.

I said softly, "It is you; you are so tall and very handsome." My husband and I were then sitting in this strange staircase that didn't lead anywhere, just watching all five kids playing a board game on the living room floor. I looked at my husband and said "I know this sounds weird, but I think I'm going to throw up! This is too much for me to take." Then I woke up feeling sick to my stomach.

The dream made me feel sad and I was mad at myself for wanting and asking for it. I cried for about two weeks. It was very hard to explain the way I was feeling. I guess it was about a year later when I was sitting in my room, pondering the dream again and I saw it in a much different light. I now saw it for the gift it was intended and I was truly honoured that my wish was granted and I saw what Ben would have looked like. Still it did have a very strange effect on me at the time I had it.

A friend in the meditation group told me that we had a Spiritualist church in our nearby town that had a service every Sunday at 11:00 am. I was extremely intrigued, so I found a babysitter for the boys that following Sunday and went to check it out.

When I first walked in I was overwhelmed with the feeling of love and comfort in the small, quaint building. The Minister, a little man in his eighties, came right up to me and gave me a big warm hug with a huge loving and gentle smile on his face. The service was wonderful, with lots of singing and tons of laughter. This was definitely nothing I had ever experienced before in a church setting!

In the service they have a part where the Minister gives messages from deceased loved ones, guardian Angels and Spirit guides. I was blessed to get a message. The Minister asked could he come to me with a message. I was open and so excited. I said "Yes, please."

He said "You have a young boy with you; I feel it is a son. He says to tell you that he knows that you have come a very long way to get to where you are now and have a lot further to go. You have recently climbed a rather large mountain and things will become easier now." He also said, "He has been trying to direct you to this church for a while now, knowing it is a place where souls on the other side can get through. I love you mom" were his parting words. I was touched by the message and did not doubt it for one second. I felt glad I had chosen to go and wanted to return to the church as often as possible.

The next Sunday I wanted to go again, but I could not find a sitter so I figured I would take the boys with me. Why not? There is no way one mom can sit between three boys at the same time and I was having trouble as to which two could sit together quietly. We started the service by singing Happy Birthday to someone there that was celebrating their special day. Next was a prayer/meditation and my youngest was still singing "Happy Birthday", I shushed him, but he just kept singing. I did not want him to disturb the others while they were meditating; I was thinking of squeezing his little knee to stop him, but knew he was the type to yell "Ouch! Mommy you hurt me, what did you do that for?"

After the service I apologized to the Minister. He said "Oh don't you worry. We love kids here and he didn't do anything wrong. Plus to be honest with you, I can still feel my mother's elbow in my ribs from so many years ago". That was comforting. The feeling I got was pure comfort and it made me feel just like I wanted to. Even I could still feel the jab to the ribs I received when I spoke out of turn or burst into laughter at church. That was so many years ago.

In late 2004 I filed for divorce. My husband contested, which meant I would need a lawyer to continue the process. As I was struggling financially I had to just let it go for the time being.

Things did start to get better for me. I continued to go to church, sometimes I took the boys and sometimes I got a little break and went alone. I also kept up with the meditation circle once a month. I had an open mind about it and found that it was softening my pain, hurt and anger. I believe even my heart was starting to open up (a little).

I kept up on my reading to broaden my mind about my Spirituality and things I had a passion for. It was then that I started to sense and feel Benjamin around me and that was well worth all the work I was doing.

Christmas of 2004 the boys and I went to my little brothers, five hours away. It was nice, even my daughter came from the big city with her boyfriend, a nine and a half hour drive for them.

The boys and I were blessed to have brought my dad back home with us for a nice five week visit. I was so grateful to have that time with my dad as we were very close. My dad passed away four months after that. He was my best friend. At this time I found out that my dad's passing brought back other passings, like Ben's and my mom's. I was so happy for my dad to go 'Home' and be with my mom, his parents, his brother and his beautiful grandson. I had never met anyone who wanted to go and meet Jesus as much as my dad. I had no regrets with him, I had always told him how much I loved him as did he tell me and I was blessed to have had the relationship with him that I did.

About five weeks later I got sick with double lumbar pneumonia. The illness lasted six weeks. I had a hard time looking after myself and the three boys during my illness. On top of all that, I was having a hard time finding anyone to help me out. Finally I found a friend, but he could not handle my youngest. Then the old "I'm responsible for everything" issue came up for me again. So I did some research on the emotional reason for the physical ailment, finding that pneumonia meant I had some suppressed grief. I then had a huge cry about my dad, which I had not done yet, I started getting better after that, and thank God. That was a hard six weeks for me and the boys.

Once I was feeling better the boys' dad showed up for a visit and it was nice for about ten minutes. He was still very angry and was blaming me for everything that he was going through. I had done enough work on myself to know I was not responsible, but I was so sad that he was yet to start healing. I asked him to leave he said "No" and it got pretty bad. At that point I had to call 911, and then he left. That was hard for all of us, the boys didn't understand their dad's behaviour and I did not either. Months went by without a word from him.

Every now and then I would hear from my daughter. It was always good to hear her voice, but also I worried as she had developed a bad drinking habit.

She was now twenty one years old and I wished there was something I could do to help her. I did my best to support her, pray for her, and send her as much healing as I could. I was very grateful that we had the communication we had. Every time she thought of her brother Ben she would drink even harder. It was hard for me to allow her to go down the path she was going, but I had to, because it was her path and not mine. I would never give up on her though, that is for sure.

About eight months later we heard from the boys' dad when he called to apologize for the last time he was here. He said he was clean and we had a nice talk. He asked since it was close to Christmas, could I bring the boys to see him two and a half hours away. I said I would, because I did not want him at my home again.

I also wanted him to see how well the boys were doing. We went and it was a good visit. He was more focused on the boys than me this time and he was clean, for the time being. He did look a lot better than the time before.

We spent the day together and the boys had a fun time with their dad, making jokes and boy stuff. I was pleased about that. We said good-bye and went on our way. That was the last time we ever saw him.

For Christmas that year the boys and I went to the big city, six hours away to see their grandparents on their dad's side. It was a nice Christmas and my daughter even showed up at grandma and grandpas for Christmas day. We had a great time and the boys were so happy to see their sister, they had missed her so much. The boys cared for and looked up to their sister so much and it was nice for me to see.

My mother-in-law and I had a great conversation, which was nice as we did not get along so well before. Now we get along much better, plus she was thrilled to see her grandsons. We spent about four days there visiting with them and my daughter and then had to get back to our lives at home.

CHAPTER NINE

Starting to grow...

Now that I was solely responsible for all of my boys, I thought it was time to do something about work, so I opened up my own cleaning business. It was long hours, hard work and finding good babysitters that I trusted was difficult. This went on for only about a year and a half when I found that I had seriously hurt my wrist. The doctor said the only way I could begin to heal it was to stop using it the way I was. This was very hard for me to accept and I just continued doing the work I was doing, because I could not see any other options at that time. Then one night I had a dream of taking my oldest boy to his graduation in a taxi cab, because I did not have the use of my right arm and it was just hanging there off my shoulder. Well, I woke in a panic and then instantly changed my mind about what I was doing to myself, my kids and our future.

Sadly we had to go back on social assistance and that was even harder for me to do. They sent me to five different career counsellors over time. They had a hard time with me as I was not one of their normal clients that do what they are told. I wanted to feed my children and have some hope for their future more than what we could get from being stuck in that position. I wanted to drive a dump truck, I figured that I could make a good enough wage to support my kids and some, but all the counsellors said "It would cost too much. You can just get a job at the local donut shop."

I decided to write a letter to our provincial government to ask them a question. "Why they could not help me out financially so I could get off social assistance for good and raise my boys on my own without any help from them?" Which I figured would be cheaper for the government in the long run. While I was waiting for a response from them I pushed forward in pursuit of finding my own way to do this.

About a month later I received a letter answering my question. Basically, they said "Because I was a single mother on social assistance, I was at the bottom of the barrel to get any further help of this type from our government" and the letter also said (This is in my words) "I was the one who got us in the situation, therefore I was to be the one to get us out".

Needless to say this was not the answer I was looking for. I have to admit I was a little angry about that response. I so wanted more for myself and my kids and was willing to work hard to get it. With that answer I was feeling somewhat degraded as all I wanted was to feed my kids and set a good example for them. Also I wanted to teach them that when a door closes there is always another one open somewhere. I continued my search for work.

In the last meeting I had with one of my career counsellors I was told to just get any job I could and they would supplement my wages. I was also told that I was to put the whole truck driving thing on the back burner. As far as I was concerned at my age I did not even have a "Back burner" when it came to earning a living and raising my boys. I left the office hopping mad and did not understanding why they had so many restriction on me when all I was wanting was to better our lives.

It turned out, that was exactly what I needed to get motivated. You see what they did not know was that I had gone ahead and gotten my airbrake ticket, thanks to my daughter giving me the money. I also had gotten my class 1 & 3 learners licenses, so I went home, got the phone book out, and phoned all the dump truck companies in our area. Low and behold one of the ready-mix companies wanted me to come and see them.

The following day I went in to see what they might have for me. I was hired so to speak. They were willing to put me in a job shadowing program, without pay, but they would teach me how to drive and I could use the dump truck for my test and when I passed I would be on the payroll and off social assistance.

I had not heard from my husband in months and was a bit concerned about the cost of putting three children in school, school fees, supplies, clothes and so on. He must have sensed something because he called at the beginning of September 2006 and for the first time I asked him for help with the money I needed for the boys. The other reason I asked for help financially was because he was working and getting paid well, not to mention the boys were his too. He surprised me by saying that he would be glad to help out with that and said he was getting paid the next day and would send me some money. I had my suspicions, but I was also quite hopeful. No money came and I have not heard from him since that call in September 2006.

Shortly after, I got a phone call from my daughter, who was not doing well emotionally. I felt bad, but I could do nothing for her. I had my own responsibilities, and needed to focus on them. So I did just that and carried on my path with the boys, sending her lots of love.

I had four girlfriends that had all lost a son. We called our group the "Lost Boys Club". We never got together, just made phone calls. I knew all of them, but only two of them knew each other. One of the ladies lost her fifteen year old son, in 1982 to a car accident. One of the others lost her thirty year old son to a drug overdose, in 1998. The third lady's son was burned in a fire in 1986. He was fifteen at the time. The last one was my friend, who lost her twenty three year old son to a tragic murder, in 2003.I had known him, a funny and nice young man who worked with and was a good friend to my daughter.

The two ladies that lost their boys over twenty years ago were both bitter and still angry. I have since lost contact with those two, but am very close to the other two.

After being trained for six months on the dump truck I went for my test and I am glad to say I passed. I was a little surprised, but happy and proud of myself. Hello, pay check and good-by social assistance! The boys were so proud of their mom. I worked very hard for that and was excited to go out on the truck by myself. But I was intimidated as well. Those are big trucks and I'm kind of a little lady for that kind of occupation. It turned out to be hard and awesome at the same time.

In the end of September 2006 I was for the first time in a lot of years (I'm talking A LOT of years......) asked out on a date by a nice man. I said "No, but thank you so much for asking and noticing me." I was too busy with my boys and our lives I could not even imagine taking the time to go to dinner with someone and to be quite frank I wasn't interested in any men other than my three sons. The other thing was that I was not feeling worthy; still feeling that I had made my bed and you know.... However He still came over and fixed the boys bikes, something I could not do as I did not have the tools, time, or knowledge. While he was fixing their bikes I made him a cup of tea and we had a nice conversation.

The Christmas of 2006 my daughter came. That was awesome and the "nice man" was kind to the kids and me, showering us with gifts. Even my boss was extra special to all of us. I found the whole thing to be quite overwhelming, as before I had struggled so much at that time of year. I still had my issues with Christmas time without my beloved Benjamin. I had to admit that things were getting easier and it truly was not that hard any more for me, in all areas in my life. I was grateful to all who helped me get this far and to myself and my incredible inner strength.

CHAPTER TEN

Discovering a new path....

The nice fellow that asked me out was still pursuing me. He was a great handyman and what single mother doesn't need help in that department? He helped me when my oven broke and watched the boys for me so I could go to my company Christmas party. It seemed he had nothing to do on Sunday mornings so I asked if he could watch the boys so I could go to church. That meant a lot to me, because I really liked going to church and it was such a handful with three young boys. He had asked me about the church I went to and I told him that it wasn't really a church so much as a gathering of loving, like-minded people.

This church that I was attending has seven principles that they go by, they are not rules, and this made me feel good.

This is a Spiritualist church, an organization dedicated to the awareness of, and the furthering of, our Spirituality, and embracing these seven principles:

1. The presence of a Universal Force.
2. The acceptance of equality of all people.
3. Communion with Spirit and the ministration of Angels.
4. The continuous existence of all souls.

5. Personal responsibility.
6. Redress for all deeds done on earth. And
7. Eternal progress open to all souls.

This was more of a way of life then a religion and it felt right for me.

The boys were really beginning to like this guy, but I was the one that was still full of hesitations. I still believed I could do everything on my own and felt I got myself where I was and I would have to get myself out. I felt I was doing quite well, thank you very much.

I was out one day with my oldest son and I said to him over a period of about fifteen through twenty minutes, "If I were to ever, maybe, sometime down the road, in the future, possibly" and I went on and on "maybe if I were to ever get like a boyfriend, somewhere down the road, do you think that he would make a good one, maybe if I decided to do something like that, down the road of course?" My son looked me right in the eye and said "DUH!" I guess that was his way of giving me his approval and that it was okay that I could move on in that area.

It was about a month after my pussyfooting around about maybe having a boyfriend that the nice man asked me to be his girlfriend. I was cautious, because it wasn't just about me; I had three young boys to consider as well. But I said yes.

All these years I could not afford a headstone for Benjamin. That was hard for me, I wanted to honour my son and I wanted people that went into that small graveyard to see who my Benjamin was somehow. I had made a big plastic Benjamin Bear for his grave and some of Ben's little friends had put some dinky toys there for him, but there was nothing to say who he was. I suppose one of the other reasons it was taking me so long to put a stone there for him was because I was being nudged in the back of my mind to make one for him, as I am a "crafty" lady. It was a very small graveyard way out in the country.

Since Benjamin's twenty-first birthday was fast approaching and I worked for a cement company, a plan for making Ben's headstone began to manifest. I asked my best friend and my new boyfriend if they would like to help me make it. They both said yes and were honoured to be part of this special gift for Ben on such a special birthday.

I went to the graveyard to get some measurements. I didn't want it too large or too small. My friend and I talked about a design and what to put on it. Meanwhile my boyfriend made a wooden form to pour the cement into. Then he had a friend make a stainless steel heart shaped plaque, which was later, engraved in kindergarten font. We went to the craft store and bought some stones that said 'JOY', 'LOVE', HAPPINESS', and 'PEACE' to put around the boarder. We also got some cement stamps for the lettering and some 24K gold leaf paint. I had been collecting granite pieces and my friend had some little round shower floor tiles and some ceramic angel wings. I purchased some silver edging to finish and complete the outer edge.

We made up the cement with a green dye in it, poured it in the form, placed the plaque and started the mosaic boarder. When we went to stamp his name, the cement had already started to set, to our dismay. All of us were tired, but we had to chip out the plaque and worded stones. Due to it setting up it was too hard to stamp his name. I looked at the time and realized it was almost 3 a.m., so we decided to call it a night, get some sleep and try again in the morning.

The next day things went a lot better. As we were waiting for it to set up again my friend chose this time to let me know what happened to her that night in September when Ben died so many years ago.

She told me how she was in her house and had heard some loud noises outside. Thinking it was a coyote she opened the door to listen and realized it was someone screaming for help. She jumped in her van and headed down the mountain, in search of the source. When she arrived at the accident she was right in the middle of her worst nightmare ever. It seemed to take forever for the ambulance and R.C.M.P. to get there. Time for her had almost stopped. She wanted to come and get me, so she spoke to an R.C.M.P. officer, once they arrived and told him that she knew the little boy's mother and wanted to go get her. He said "No, not yet." Time seemed to tick and tick so slowly for her then. She told the officer that she could not wait and was going to get the boy's mother. "No!" is what he said again. Since she was in shock she could not understand why the wait, she couldn't stand it any longer and jumped in her van to head down the mountain.

The officer leaped out in front of her and again repeated "NO!" She stuck her head out the window and said "I'm going to get his mom and if you don't get out of the way I'll hit you!" We later found out that the R.C.M.P. did not want her to get me because they simply were not ready to deal with what might be a traumatic scene.

After the evening was over she went home alone, still in shock and numb all over. She had no one to support her but kept it from me so I could grieve my son and go through my process. She had kept this painful secret for over sixteen years. Well, we were quite the sight, the two of us sitting on my driveway hugging, crying and covered in cement.

My heart broke again, but this time for my dear friend and the trauma she went through that same night.

After the stone was done we had to put a cement sealer on it to protect it from the weather. I had gotten an epoxy sealer, my boyfriend mixed it up and poured it on. It was a Friday morning and we were to place the stone on Sunday afternoon. We both left for work. On our return home on Friday evening we went to the garage to reveal the beautiful finished product. I was devastated to see that the sealer had gone all milky. It was ruined. I was beyond up set.

I looked at my boyfriend and said "I'm going to town." I got in my car and drove. I couldn't cry I just was in a daze. I so wanted the stone to be perfect, because it was for such a special reason and for such a special boy. We just couldn't do another one in time, there was no way. I continued to drive aimlessly around until about two hours later I returned to find my boyfriend sitting on the hard cement floor in the garage with the smallest screwdriver I've ever seen, picking off the milky sealer, tiny bit by tiny bit. What patience this guy has, I thought.

I went in the house to fix dinner; fed the boys and dished some up to take out to my boyfriend. He ate and picked, ate and picked at the sealer. I started doing the same.

Sometime later he told me I should go in the house and go to bed, but I refused and kept on picking. I picked until I fell asleep. This time I listened, and went to bed. But he stayed out there patiently picking until it was all off, for ten hours total he sat there. What a trooper I had!

On Sunday after the church service we went to the graveyard to place the headstone. We were very blessed to have our Minister make the one hour drive out there to do an incredible 'Celebration of life' for my Benjamin's twenty-first birthday. It was beautiful, my little brother came; also in attendance was my daughter, my three sons, my best friend and my boyfriend. To my surprise the man that was there so many years ago when we buried Ben was able to come. He let the kids into the church to ring the church bell. How precious is that?

Not long after Ben's birthday I approached our Minister and asked him what it would take for me to become a Minister for the Spiritualist church. I most definitely had some kind of calling to do this work together with a huge passion in my heart. He was overjoyed to take me under his wing. It didn't take me long to get started on the process of becoming a Minister and opening my heart up to Spirit. More books to read. This required me to not only open my heart, but also my mind. This was all very new to me and not the way I was raised. The more I read and the more I opened my mind the more sense it all made to me.

My boyfriend asked the boys and me to move in with him. We said in unison "YES!" This was the best move I was to make in the last sixteen years. He had a beautiful little house out in the mountains with the most spectacular view I had ever seen around these parts. I had two months to move which was ample time. It was an easy move and we were only a ten minute drive from where I laid my precious son to rest, but I know he has made every one of the moves with me.

I had not heard from the kids' dad in quite some time, so I continued to send loving and healing Angels to be by his side. I really prayed he could heal, not for me not even for the kids, but for himself. I often sent him forgiveness; I was now learning how important forgiveness was in the healing process for me.

CHAPTER ELEVEN

Finally working out some stuff....

Attending church every Sunday now, participating in the Tuesday night meditation circles and lots more reading brought me to a better understanding of who I really am. I have been able to open up both my mind and my heart. I now realize that I have grown so much and that I have to accept the person I was, the person I am and the person I am becoming. Learning more and more about forgiveness has been a huge bonus in my life. Learning about forgiveness is one thing, practising it is another, but allowing forgiveness to heal is again a whole different thing. Self-forgiveness is the key and the best place to start, for me anyway.

My boyfriend is such a loving, kind and patient man, he has taught me so much without even knowing it. He is also very attentive to me and that has been a hard thing for me to get used to. It may sound weird, but I have always been the type of person that thought "I have to do everything and do it myself". However I am learning to adjust and allow him and others to help me, sometimes. It has been a difficult, long and ongoing process. I am a giving person, but have a tendency to put myself last. Now that is all changing and I have to step out of that box.

Like I said I know I have come a long way, but I still get sad, upset and don't fully understand the whole thing and how I can keep breathing. I did have a great example sixteen years ago when I went to my grandfather's funeral. My grandfather's girlfriend was sitting all alone and I went to talk to her. As she was legally blind I announced myself and sat down beside her. She put her hand on my lap and said "Tell me about your boy and what happened to him."

I began my story that I had told so many times. She instantly had a stream of tears running down her checks, and then said to me "I'm not crying for your boy, I'm crying for my boys that I lost in 1940 and 1970. I just want you to know that this is something that you will carry with you until your journey ends on the earth plain and you are reunited with him on the other side."

I learned that day that tears, sadness and anger could happen at any time and for no reason at all, but for good reason too. I have always remembered what she said to me that day.

I would like to tell you a little bit about this beautiful woman and her hardships. She passed away in 1999 at the age of 94 years. She did so much in her life; enough to write a book which she did. She even wrote a couple of them. She lived in the prairies in a small house way out in the bush, a true pioneer. When she was in her early twenties she was home alone and went into labour with her first child, having a 10lb. 2oz. baby boy all by herself. Two years later she had a friend over for tea when she went into labour with her second child. Her friend scooted the two year old outside to play while the two of them delivered her second son at 11lb. 4oz.

Meanwhile outside the young boy had tripped and fallen head first into a puddle and drowned. About thirty years later her other son with his two teenage kids where traveling to see her for Christmas, hit some black ice, went off the road into a river and all three of them drowned. I still wonder how much one can take. Some have huge strength and others maybe not. I believe the hardest test of faith, on the earth plain, is losing a child.

Benjamin's twenty-third birthday was upon us already and it happened to be one of the hard ones for me. Then I remembered what my friend said to me six years before, so I asked myself what had happened to me when I was twenty-three? That was the year Ben was born and came into my life. Funny as it seems, that made me feel a bit better.

One of the Ministers from the church called me that morning to see how I was doing. So I was honest with her and said "Not that great." I told her that I was really sad and feeling a little guilty. I was surprised at myself for using the word guilty. It wasn't because of any responsibility I had or didn't have about Ben's passing. It was more about wondering what happened to his dad who took such a nose dive and didn't seem to come back up.

And Ben's sister and her drinking, I was so sad for both of them. I guess the guilt was coming from, "Was it okay for me to be doing as well as I was? Was it really alright for me? It didn't seem like it was okay for Ben's dad and sister, why was it okay for me?" That night I said a prayer to Ben and I truly felt his reassurance that it was just fine by him and should be okay for me.

This led me to research 'Survivors Guilt' on the internet. This sure explained my daughters' behaviour. Subconsciously she doesn't think that it was fair to have a good joyful life when her brother cannot. I had to admit this has also been an issue for me. That's why I was wondering if I was allowed to be happy. I believe this is quite common in parents and surviving siblings. Here was a new mission for me. I spent the next year gathering information and trying to shed any 'Survivors Guilt' that I might have.

CHAPTER TWELVE

Allowing my passion to come through....

I started a Counselling/Hypnotherapy course to take up some of my time while the boys were at school. I have always been interested and had a passion in counselling and helping people and feel I have had the life experience to help a variety of people. I also continued studying for the Ministry.

I was still in the process of getting my divorce finalized. I had a good lawyer and all the ends were completely tied up on what would have been our twenty-sixth wedding anniversary. A friend of mine said she thought that was neat and tidy. I was married for exactly twenty-six years. The divorce felt fairly good, but I was hoping it would feel exhilarating, as well as feeling like that chapter of my life was finally closed.

When I spoke earlier about, "How hard does the work have to be?" Well, staying married to him was just too much work for me and I felt that my soul was being depleted. When Ben passed away and I read the first book about losing a child, in 1990 the statistics said that parents that lost a child had a seventy-five percent chance of divorcing. I did not want to be in the majority, but just had to if I wanted to continue to grow and heal. In 2009 the statistics went up to ninety-five percent, due to how much people change under so much devastation and trauma. I am very hopeful for that five percent because true love should pull us through anything and the fact that only five percent survive makes me feel so sad. I guess it was not strong enough for us, but where that path led me has been worth the journey.

Much to my surprise, shortly after my divorce was finalized my boyfriend proposed to me. Wow! There was someone who wanted to take me, all my kids and our heavy baggage too. He was either crazy or very much in love with us. I happily accepted. I then asked him if I could tell the boys, but he said he would rather do it when he took us all out for dinner. I was so excited and couldn't wait to see the expressions' on their faces.

We were through our meal and he was just finishing up his desert when I elbowed him and quietly asked "Are you going to talk to the boys or what?"

He looked at me and said "I did, when you went to the bathroom!" He had a big smile on his face.

"WHAT? You did it without me?" I was shocked; the boys were looking at me with no expressions at all on their faces, so I could not pick up on anything. I have to say I was quite disappointed that I didn't see their faces or hear what they had to say. The boys and I had done so much growing together and I felt it was important to me. So I said "Well what did they say?" He told me that it was all positive, but I wanted more and needed more than that. I looked him right in the eye and said "AND?"

He just laughed a little and began telling me what their responses were. The youngest said, "HURRAY! We finally have a dad." He doesn't really remember his father, but he surely missed having one in his life and he let me know that all the time.

The next one said "That would be okay with me." His response was a bit of a surprise as he is the family comedian, but later when he was asked to be one of the best men his reply was "Oh sure, I would love to be your B.M." giggle, giggle!

The oldest of the three said "I would really like that." This was heart-warming for me as he is the one always looking out for his mom. So I guessed all was well. I just had to wait for my daughter to call, so I could tell her.

While I was busy studying my mid-terms for my counselling/hypnotherapy course my husband-to-be (with a little help from the boys), built an office on the side of our house. I have a small fountain and pond in the room, but my favourite thing is the curtain rod holders which are hand-carved wooden Angel wings, absolutely immaculate. What a wonderful space for me and the energy is so beautiful and loving. That is where I was while writing this section of my book. I have been so blessed, not just to have a man like this in my life, but his connection to the boys is awesome. I could not ask for anything more.

That summer of 2009 the kids were twenty-four, fourteen, twelve and eight years old. We were married in our front yard overlooking the beautiful lake in the company of the majestic mountains and Mother Nature. It was wonderful and ever so enchanting. We had two of the Ministers from our church do the ceremony.

We wrote our own vows and there were some moist eyes, in the lawn chairs behind us, when my new husband said how blessed he was to be welcomed into the family, listing all the kids including Ben. That was so special for me, my daughter, my little brother who gave me away and my best friend who was my maid of honour, standing beside me as she had done for the last eighteen years.

As beautiful as the wedding was I realized that I still had a huge hole in my heart and wondered if it would ever be filled. I am a happy person and laugh lots, but I experience very little joy when it comes to my emotions. Something I would have to look into, but sooner than later for my new husband and four children. I looked into it and found that happiness is on the outside, that is what others see, but joy is inside where there was more work for me.

My daughter stayed for about ten days after the wedding. One day she decided to drive to the graveyard to sit with Benjamin. We know he is not there, but the physical part that his dad and I had a great deal in making was there. When my daughter came back a couple of hours later I could smell the booze, but I stayed silent. With tear filled eyes she said "Mom, I so broke down and I would have still been there lying next to him if it wasn't for the ants all over. Mom I realized that I have not dealt with the loss of Ben yet and I couldn't handle it so I bought a small bottle and drank the whole thing." My heart was breaking for her and for myself, still having a hard time with her drinking.

So we sat together and spoke about where she was in all of this and why she continued to have such a hard time, just as though everything happened yesterday. I had to tell her that I felt she had not really started to heal yet, that she was blocking the healing every time she drank, using that same excuse over and over again. She said "But it's been eighteen years mom. What do I do?"

"Well", I began "I believe you have to stop covering up your feelings with booze and allow them to surface so you can feel them and then move through them. It is hard, but that is the first step and the first step is the hardest, then it only gets better after that. You know honey they say that time heals, but I don't believe that. I feel that it is what we do in that time that determines how fast or slow we heal. You, your dad and I all have had the same amount of time and we are all in three different places."

Since that day she has slowed her drinking down quite a bit, but has not stopped completely. I have so much faith in her and of course an incredible yearning for her to get on her path of healing. She is a wonderful soul with a compassionate heart and special mission in this life time. I just know that in my heart.

Shortly after my daughter left for home, I got back to my studies. The Ministry is much more a way of life than anything else, which means my studies for that are ongoing. I did have to continue studying my counselling/hypnotherapy. I worked hard on my schooling and graduated as an A plus student. I was surprised, but my husband was not, he had incredible faith in me.

One Sunday at church I found myself looking around at all the new people and realized that a lot of them had lost a child. I was grateful they had found our church; as it had helped me so much. I feel that Spiritualism had brought me from a very dark, unfeeling and damp cave like existence to a bright, warm, sunny and loving life. I believe, for me anyway, that it is a much healthier way to live. You have to keep living after you have lost a child so wouldn't you want it to be sunny instead of dark? My heart breaks when I consider that there are parents out there that think there is no life after death. I don't know how they continue to live or breathe for that matter. I don't feel that I am the only one that has an unbreakable connection with my son; I feel we all have this gift.

I feel that my belief, that life goes on after the transition of death, has had everything to do with blowing that sunny breath into my lungs for me. It is the only explanation I can come up with. I know that we all need to experience our own lives in our own way and have our individual paths to follow, because we are all different with different needs.

My wish to anyone who has lost a loved one and especially a child is that they find a way, anyway to know that they are still close to us. Maybe one day to be able to feel their presence by your side, rather than waiting until you meet again on the other side. It has brought me so much loving comfort and great strength.

CHAPTER THIRTEEN

The breath is coming easier now....

I have so much gratitude for the church, its members and Spiritualism. Opening up my heart and mind to Spirit, a higher power and the Angels, has simply brought me a lot of much needed peace. I am helped every day if I ask when previously I didn't even feel worthy to ask. I thought I had to do everything on my own. Before that I didn't know we could ask for help from a higher Spirit. The fear of death, which stifles most of mankind, is not near as heavy for me anymore. I feel there is no death, just a passing from one realm to the other and the continuation of our soul's growth.

Another thing that has been a tremendous help to me is meditating. At our meditation circles the messages from our loved ones, Angels and guides are usually short, but profound and authentic. According to what I have learned, when a soul wants to communicate with us they have to lower their vibrations to do so. When we meditate and are in alignment we raise our vibrations, that way we can meet in the middle and make it easier for everyone.

My dream in all of this is to meet up with Benjamin and my parents in a meditation. It does not happen very often, but on occasion it does. I don't meditate as much as I could or would like to. One day I just happened to have the time and had a very nice meditation to try out.

In this particular meditation you get comfortable, relax (maybe some soft music in the background if you prefer) and imagine yourself walking in a beautiful and sunny green meadow. You hear off in the distance a babbling brook and you follow the sound. When you arrive at the source of the water you come upon a bridge. You start walking onto the bridge until you get to the middle, then look down at your reflection and just observe it for a moment. At the other end of the bridge is your Guardian Angel waiting for you. You walk hand in hand with your Angel for a little while talking or just being silent in each other's company.

Your Angel leads you to an archway with ivy all around it; it is the entrance to a heavenly garden more beautiful than you have ever seen. Your Angel waits at the archway for you and you go into the garden. You follow the path to a huge tree, at the base of the tree there is a bench and you sit down. Soon someone from the other side, a loved one or Guide will join you. You may have a conversation with them or just sit quietly and enjoy their loving light and energy. After a little while they just disappear and you know it is time to leave, but remember that you can return to your special garden any time you would like just by going into a meditative state.

Back at the archway you meet your awaiting Angel and you are gently guided back to the bridge. You say goodbye and thank you to your Angel, with a loving hug, as you walk up onto the bridge you stop again and have a look at your reflection. This time see if you can notice how much brighter you look, then through the meadow and back into your body. At this point you might want to just lie there and assimilate your experience of this heavenly journey or you may also want to write down what you have gained or brought back with you.

When I had the opportunity to do this meditation, this is what happened for me. After I was led to the garden by my Angel I sat on the bench and waited, then my dear mother showed up. She pointed over to the other end of the garden to a beautiful gazebo and offered her hand to take me there. There was an incredible table set up for a meal. My grandmother was there as well. My mom and I sat down with her and there was one chair left. It was to be filled by Ben. Within a second there he was sitting with all of us. There was no words said just loving thoughts. Soon some Angels served us a wonderful meal and we ate in peaceful silence.

A short while later I had to break the silence to say how spectacular the food was and how I had never before experience anything that tasted so incredible. Benjamin said "I cooked it mom, that's what I do here and I love it. I'm glad you enjoyed it." Then everything went misty and my mom led me back to my Angel. I cannot even begin to tell you what that was like for me.

I was feeling so much better at this point in my life, but still I had this mysterious lack of joy. I guess I felt it was not fair to Ben, my daughter or my ex-husband for me to have a joyful life. I felt I had been sentenced eighteen years ago to live the rest of my life without joy. Even with my three boys and new wonderful husband and the career of my passion I felt badly that I was not able to express the joy that I should have been feeling. Something was telling me I was not allowed to go there.

After admitting this to myself again, I thought I better start working on it. It is such hard work and it's sad, but I pushed forward anyways. I decided to get together with a man from our church that lost his granddaughter; she was the love of his life. He is a hypnotherapist also and I asked if he could help me with my lack of joy issue.

He put me in a trance and I was blessed to meet up with Ben in that state of mind. The first thing Ben said to me was "Mom you have no idea what joy I am experiencing where I am now, so there is no need for you to hold back. If you can't do it for yourself you have to do it for my sister and especially for my three little brothers who still have lots of growing and learning to do. They need to be guided into a joyful life, they deserve it. You are their mother and their teacher, you have to show them and it must be authentic. I know you can do it mom you have already come such a long way and I am so proud of you and I will always love you and help you as much as I can from here." As he began to fade I heard him say "It is okay for you to feel joyful mom, it is so okay!"

When I came out of the trance I said with moist eyes, "That was so beautiful, but something tells me it's just not that easy."

My friend said "Yes, it is that easy, just believe it is." I don't know why I still doubt it, but I do. Yes, I have come a long way in the last eighteen years, but there is still such a big hole and it is still quite painful at times. Then I remembered what my grandfather's girlfriend told me about losing her sons, "It never goes away!" Maybe I need to accept that and continue to do the best I can.

I am reading books about Angels and communicating with Spirit all the time now, I love to learn more about my passions in life. I always send healing love to my daughter and her dad. In September 2009 my daughter came to visit and introduced us to her new boyfriend. My husband and I both liked him right away, nice energy. They have something in common as well; they have both lost a sibling. His sister was murdered in 2005.

I know my daughter loves to go to our church, so I asked if they would like to join us one Sunday. He said he would love to come and was quite interested in it. Now every time they come out here he asks if we are going to church and can they come.

I had taken up doing Angel card readings some years ago. Even my husband reads them. I have to admit he is very good due to not having a hard time getting his ego out of the way. In September I gave my daughter a reading and it was one of the most incredible things that has happened to me. I give people messages at church from Spirit and I am getting better, because I allow Spirit to come through me and I just trust, but this was different. In the reading for my daughter with the second card out of three, I held it in my hands, closed my eyes and took a deep breath. All of a sudden I had this overwhelming feeling that Ben was with me. Streams of tears flowed down my cheeks. When my daughter noticed the tears she asked, "What's wrong mom?"

I said "Nothing is wrong, I just feel Ben so strongly here right now it's a bit overwhelming, but at the same time it's so beautiful." She told me that I didn't have to continue if I didn't want to, but I did want to, it was such an incredible feeling. I said "Oh yes I do, your brother has a very profound message for you and these are his words not mine."

This is what he is telling me to say "Tell my sister I watch her lots and sometimes I want to shake her. I want to shake her out of it. I wish she could see the beautiful soul within her that I see. She is a wonderful and compassionate person, but when she drinks it distorts her thinking and makes her block her feelings. Also when she is like that she cannot hear the Angelic guidance that is trying to help her. She needs to stop completely to get on the path to heal and the path is made of pure love."

"Believe me honey," I said "This is coming straight from Ben."

That was an incredible thing for me and I was honoured that he came to me or I should say through me for his sister. All I can say is that it was a wonderful gift for both of us. I was a little concerned that my daughter would not believe me or think it was authentic, but I'm sure my tears gave her a big clue. She said that it was a great message, but I still wondered.

CHAPTER FOURTEEN

Supporting now, but still learning....

One day I was at church and I was asked by one of our newcomers, who had just lost her twenty year old son, if I could start a support group for parents. I said yes and was honoured that she asked me. I have to admit that I was a little intimidated since I'd never even been to a support group let alone run one, but I knew I could trust Spirit to guide me.

Our first support group meeting was great. There were only four of us, but we found that because we were all on common ground it felt good. We were help for each other; each of us had experienced hell in our own way and was able to share that without judgement. We had all lost a son and all the boys would have been around the same age. They were all born between 1986 -1990. The difference for me was that they all lost their sons within the last year.

One of the ladies that attended had lost two boys in separate incidents, her first boy passed years before then she lost her nineteen year old to a car accident. The man that came had just lost his nineteen year old to a car accident as well. The other lady's boy passed due to a cliff diving accident. We were on more common ground then we first realized. I believe the meetings turned out to be exactly as they were meant to be.

When you have lost a child all you want to do is talk about them and your experience. This can be hard and taxing on our family and friends to listen to all the time. They cannot feel your pain nor should they. Our group did not have this problem and it was nice for each of us to listen from a knowing heart. I remember when I was first grieving and people would say to me "I'm so sorry, I can't even imagine what you are going through."

I would say "Why would you, why would anyone imagine such a thing?" I always wondered why someone would say that, it kind of made me mad at the time. That may sound weird, but it's just one of things that bugged me and I know it was said with good intentions and people do have a hard time knowing what to say. I had a friend that was honest; she just looked at me and said "I don't know what to say."

While I was writing this I realized that it was not these people or the statement that made me angry, it was misplaced anger I had towards God for taking my boy. This surprised me, so I did a bit of inner work and felt better about it all.

Getting grief counselling is good for some people, but they are timed sessions and the chances of the counsellor having lost a child are poor, thank goodness. I know that the counselling my daughter got so many years ago was good for her. I am not knocking it. Like I said it is good for some and maybe not for others.

I am a trained counsellor; I have found it more effective for me to work with people in a situation that I have experienced in my own life. I can still counsel someone in a situation that I have not experienced, but that is what I went to school for.

An interesting thing that I recently learned, although I'm sure I knew subconsciously years ago, is that when you lose a child you subconsciously attract others who have had the same experience. I think it's our broken hearts that silently yearn to share with someone in the same boat. I believe our hearts send the message to our subconscious minds then it synchronisticly begins to happen. This is a good thing I'm sure because if I personally left it up to my conscious mind I would have continued to struggle on my own, maybe that's why recovering from personal tragedy can be so hard for some people. We do not have to ever go it alone. There is always someone that has gone through a similar situation, not to mention all the help we have from the other side. Our guides and Angels never leave our side. We just need to know that and ask for their help.

It has been over eighteen years since Ben passed and I have been pushed and nudged in all kinds of directions to help others. This is why when I had the opportunity to go to school for a counselling hypnotherapist I grabbed it as fast as I could. This is also the reason I was excited to start the support group, but who knew while I was helping people that I would find some help for myself, when I wasn't even looking. That's one of the beautiful things about helping others, it comes back tenfold. I feel very blessed for such a healing gift that goes both ways.

One of the most important things for me whether in my support group, meditation circles, church services or therapy sessions is for people to feel completely safe, heard and not judged. Particularly in the support group, we are all putting our hearts out on the table, very vulnerable and if someone did not feel safe, it could block the healing process. If we had someone in the group that was loud and annoying or disrespectful, others would not feel safe to share. I surely don't want to judge anyone and all people deserve to have help but at the same time it must be safe in any kind of group. When counselling individuals it is different.

I host a meditation circle in my beautiful office twice a month, the purpose is to develop a connection to Spirit and if someone feels unsafe or judged it can block the progress of all the members.

One of the things we spoke about at the first support group meeting was the raising of our other children. We are a different breed; we become much more protective, because God forbid we have to go through that again. Even the thought can be quite sickening to us.

I always told my daughter that she had to be where she said she was going to be or I would worry myself sick and she could not put me through that. I don't know if that's selfish of a parent? Don't we have to let them live with normal boundaries? We cannot guilt our children out, can we?

I look back at times like when she missed the bus after school when she was seven years old and when she ran away from home and I didn't know where she was for two and a half months. The feelings just about killed me. I told her over and over again that she could not do that to me, because I relived the accident all over.

Did I guilt her out? Am I responsible for her slower progress in healing and possibly her drinking? I do not know the answers to these questions and I wish I did. We have to live and learn I suppose. We don't get an instruction manual on how to raise our kids the perfect way to benefit all involved, nor is there a book that tells us how to raise a child after you have lost one, had your heart broken beyond repair, and then have to continue to live. No there are no such manuals out there. We just have to live and learn to the best of our ability.

The support goes on and so does the learning. One of the ladies in the group mentioned that her number one pet peeve was when people said "I know how you are feeling." Or worse "I know how you feel because I just lost my ten-year-old cat."

It is true; we don't know how someone else is feeling, because we are all so different. I have said this before we can show empathy, but we just do not know how they really feel.

The whole topic reminded me of a sympathy card I got a couple of days after the funeral; on the front of it were beautiful flowers. It was a lovely card, but it said "I know what you are going through." Well before I opened it I was angry and said quite loudly, "Who the hell is this from? Who the hell thinks they know what I feel? Nobody has any idea." I opened the card to see it was from one of the ladies who was years later in our "lost boys telephone club". So we talked about that and how there is always different circumstances.

Originally this is where I was going to end my story, but some other things have come up in the time of my typing that I feel are important.

CHAPTER FIFTEEN

There is a light at the end of the tunnel...

When talking to a friend one day about my daughter and how worried I was about her drinking, my friend said "You, of all people know what kind of energy you are sending out there when you talk like that, don't you?" I did not have to think long about what she meant and decided right then and there to change. Now it was time to start seeing her getting better by sending out positive and loving energy instead of negative.

In mid May 2010, one morning my daughter called, she sounded okay, in the beginning of our conversation. We spent four hours on the phone and by the end of the call she was drunk. She did a lot of crying and was extremely hard on herself. I told her that I was scared that she might die from her drinking. Then she asked if it really frightened me? I replied that it almost scared me to death, she was very surprised, so was I. I was amazed that she didn't know how much I loved and cared about her and her life.

That's when I said "Enough is enough, you have got a problem and you desperately need to get some help and get it soon and I'm saying this because of how much I love you." She then admitted that she truly did have a problem and needed help to stop.

I finally asked her if she could make a promise to herself to start becoming the beautiful person she really was. She could not do that, her confidence level was so low and she just did not feel worthy. I asked if maybe she could make that promise to me. After some more tears she said "I think I can do that mom."

"What about your brother Ben, can you promise him that you will?" I asked. More than a minute later I got a very quiet yes from her. "Okay what about you now?" I asked again.

After ten minutes of tears and some loving coaxing from me she said "Yes I can." Then she said "I will go get some help, maybe early next week, because I'm still looking for a job." I told her that there was no time like the present and that tomorrow would be better.

The next day she did not go for help, because of some personal obligations, but the following day she did. She ended up going to the same detoxification centre that I did so many years ago. She went in May, the same month as myself, and she was the same age almost exactly as our birthdays are only a week apart. I thought that was synchronistic and it gave me hope.

She called me every second day. She was to be in there for seven days, but she chose to stay for ten, thinking the extra time would be helpful.

I spent many hours on the phone with her boyfriend trying to help him understand her addiction and I believe my stories of my own addictions were helpful to him. He said he was grateful for our conversations.

After the ten days she decided it wasn't enough for her so she signed herself into a twenty-eight day recovery program.

Its location was a five hour drive from their home. I was so happy for her and I was beginning to see a light at the end of the tunnel. I loved her so much and could see her incredible potential, and I think she was starting to see it now as well, because her perception was not as distorted as before. I could not have asked for more.

I did not receive any phone calls from her while she was in the recovery centre, but she did call her boyfriend a couple of times, then he called me and let me know how she was doing. He was only able to go see her twice in that whole time and I know that was hard for him, but he knew it would all be worth it when she came home.

I got a phone call from him one day and he said "It would be nice if you came with me to pick her up on her graduation day." I said I would talk to my husband about it and call him back later that day.

I realized that the day she was getting out was really special, as it was also Benjamin's twenty-fourth birthday. What a wonderful way to change that day around for both of us. I spoke to my husband and it was all going to work out fine for me to leave for a couple of days. I phoned her boyfriend and told him it was a go and not to tell her, because I wanted it to be a surprise. I really felt that she didn't know how much I supported her and what she was going through. I remember when I came home after my stay in a place like that. The loving support of friends and family was vitally important.

On a Thursday afternoon I left for my six hour drive to their home. I was so excited to see my real daughter again.

Her boyfriend and I set off the next morning at 2:30 am to make the five hour journey to get her. We had a nice drive and conversation. He was so excited and a little anxious and I didn't blame him. He didn't know what to expect, but knew she was probably not the same girl he dropped off four weeks earlier.

We arrived early so we had breakfast and did some deep breathing exercises. The ceremony for her and her twenty-eight day group was to start at 9:00am. When we pulled up at the recovery centre I decided to hide behind the main doors so I could jump out and surprise her. I could hear her coming and then hugging her man. He said "I have a surprise for you!" That was my cue to come out from my hiding place.

When she saw me she ran into my outreached arms with tear filled eyes and said "Mommy! I'm so glad you're here."

Hearing her speak in front of the group about her experiences and the beginning of her recovery was awesome and I have to admit it took me back in time. She looked so healthy and beautiful, a time I had so looked forward to, and I was a very proud mother and sat there with a huge grin on my face.

On the long ride home she was excited to tell us about all the things she had learned and all the new tools she had gotten to keep her on her path to recovery. She read us a letter that she had to write to her addiction. Apparently, she was the only one who thanked her addiction for the lessons it taught her. Then there was the letter to her dad. It was hard for me to hear, but I was incredibly grateful that she had gotten that down on paper and out of her. I truly believe that writing things out is a wonderful way to release. She told us about an exercise were you draw an egg shape on a piece of paper. This was called a "Cause and Effect egg". Inside the egg was the cause, you wrote down all the things you are or have become and on the outside of the egg was the effect, who and how you got there. She said at first she was having trouble thinking what to write down about me, her mother. I knew that would be hard because she had to think back so far, due to how much I had changed, but at the same time I knew what I was accountable for. She didn't have any problem writing stuff down in the section about fathers. Then she got to mothers and she said it just all flowed out. She wrote that I was a major victim and extremely co-dependent. I felt quite small, but only for a moment as I was so proud of her digging that deep and getting it out.

I spent the rest of Friday and all of Saturday with them. I was elated by her progress and who she was now able to become; the real loving beautiful person that I saw deep within her.

I asked her if she would maybe like a card reading, she hesitated a little due to the last reading I gave her. She said "That would be nice mom". In the reading my mom, her grandmother came with a message of being by her side to help her with her healing. My mother was a nurse and she had passed five years before my daughter was born. My mom said she would stay with her granddaughter until she was no longer needed, we both found that quite comforting. Next, Ben came in quickly to say that he knew she could do it and it was nice to see his real sister again. He also mentioned how proud he was to be able to watch her blossom into the beautiful flower that he has always seen beneath her old mask. One more message came, which was from my dad. He was standing there with a rag, saying that he would keep all of her new tools clean and shiny for her. My father was a very clean mechanic. I think she enjoyed that reading much better and was completely comfortable and excited knowing they were all there to help her.

I left the next morning at 4:30 am so I could make it back for church and our A.G.M. I felt confident that all would be well; nevertheless I left Angels to help with all the new adjustments to come. I knew that they both had lots of their own Angels, but I thought it wouldn't hurt if they had a few more.

Leaving and sending Angels to or for someone is an easy and wonderful quality to have. I believe everyone has it if they want to access it. What you do, is imagine Angels in your mind's eye. See and feel them, then ask them to go to that person and with the incredible power of your heart you see them go and trust in the process. I do this with my husband, kids and friends quite often. I have even sent them across the world. It is all about believing and trusting.

CHAPTER SIXTEEN

Some sad news....

At the end of June 2010 my husband received a phone call from his closest friend. Through tears and much pain his friend said that their son had gone missing from a rafting trip. He had fallen in the full raging river and could not get out. He was their only child and he was twenty years old. I had met him only twice and he seemed like a nice young man, smart handsome and full of life.

This was terrible news. He was their whole world. It also affected my husband who was very close to his friend. And as per usual it brought up stuff for me as well; I was so heartbroken for them. When we went to their home the energy was so thick with sadness it nearly turned my stomach. I wanted to help them both, but I could do nothing but listen. I guess that was a form of help.

My husband went searching down at the river for the first two days as were the R.C.M.P. and Search and Rescue teams, but there was no sign of him. Everyone had the highest hopes that he was able to get out and was maybe disoriented, in shock and possibly just lost in the forest.

My husband asked me if I wanted to come with him on the third day. My first response was an excuse due to my fears.

"I can't. I promised to bake the boys a pie tomorrow." He said that was fine, but he was going to try again anyway. I was terrified to go searching. What if we found his body? What if we didn't? So many things went through my mind at the time. I felt I needed a little bit of quiet time.

I suddenly realized that in becoming a Minister, I might have to do some things in the future that I was afraid of or didn't want to do, but what changed my mind and made me decide to go, was thinking about not wanting his dad to find him. No parent should have to go through that. So together my husband and I went the next day and searched up and down the river all day, but to no avail.

His body was recovered fifteen days later. I believe that brought some closure to his mother, but his dad had such a hard time with that. Did he have too much hope that his son got out of the water? How could you not?

A couple of days later I was driving and had the radio on listening to the local news, which is rare for me, when they mentioned that a few young adults were partying at the same river and a girl fell in. The other kids worked tirelessly to get her out, but they could not. Apparently she was found the next morning, she managed to get out. She was cold and scared, but alive. I didn't tell anyone and had hoped that my husband's friends did not hear it. It made me wonder "Why her?" which I was truly grateful for, but why not him? Nothing like a tragedy makes one question their faith so deeply.

My husband and I went to the Celebration of Life and it was beautiful if you can say that. Lots of young adults and incredible words from his friends about what kind of a guy he was. It was so hard for his parents; they were the kind of people that had his friends and half the neighbourhood over at their place all the time. The journey ahead looked very hard, quiet and lonely. My heartfelt thoughts went to them both.

One evening my husband said he had a question for me from his friend and his wife. They wanted to give us their sons snowmobile for our boys. They were a little afraid to ask me as it is so close to a dirt bike.

I had to think about that. Part of me thought that we had gotten along just fine without one for many years, but there was the other part of me, that was honoured that they would want to pass it down to our boys. Then something a friend said to me about a year earlier came up in my mind. He said that maybe restricting my boys from never going on a dirt bike might not be a good idea. He suggested that one day one of the boys may go on a dirt bike, because all their friends are and then possibly get hurt, due to having had no experience. I for sure didn't want anything like that to happen. It really is hard to know what to do. I thought about it some more.

Later my husband told me he had grown up with a snowmobile and knew a lot about them. I swallowed hard and said that we would take it. It was hard for me to make that decision. At the time, I had no idea how useful it would be that coming winter. We had a tremendous amount of snow and because we live so far out sometimes our road does not get ploughed for two or three days. So there were a lot of days we were unable to drive the boys to the bus stop for school or pick them up afterwards. Needless to say the snowmobile came in very handy that year and I was grateful.

My husband gave lessons to the two older boys how to operate the machine and they loved it. For me it was a lesson on getting past some of my old issues. However when my oldest son came in from his first solo trip the look of excitement in his eyes was priceless and reminded me that as parents we have to loosen the leash for their own growth as hard as it might be. The oldest was going to get his driver's licence this year and I was going to have to deal with that whether I liked it or not.

I know this was a difficult thing to do for me, but gradually through time I have had to let go and will have more situations in the future, so I can allow and encourage the boys to grow and be responsible.

CHAPTER SEVENTEEN

My ordination....

The day had come, July 19th 2010, for my ordination. I was excited and only a little nervous. I knew how hard I had worked for this and acknowledged my struggles with my emotional baggage. I was feeling pretty good that I was becoming a Minister!

My daughter came and stayed almost three weeks. We thoroughly enjoyed her visit. She mentioned to me how nice it was to see everyone and everything with new and clear eyes. She also realized that we all loved her very much for who she really is. She pulled me aside to tell me through moist eyes how proud she was of me and that I was an inspiration to her and her future.

My little brother was able to come with his son and that meant the world to me as well, I had not seen them for a year, since my wedding.

Well it was a gorgeous day as we left for the church. I was a bit nervous, but not too bad. The people at the church are like family, so loving and non-judgemental. They too were so proud of me. I truly felt both my parents with me and heard them tell me how much they loved me and who I had become. We normally have between forty and fifty people at a service and on my special day we had seventy seven that came in my honour. I was very pleased.

The ceremony was beautiful and the music and singing was heavenly. After, I was presented with my purple Stoll and badge that showed I was now a Reverend Minister. I had to give a fifteen to twenty minute acceptance speech. I was nervous as all eyes were just on me.

First I expressed my gratitude toward all my Angels, Guides and Spirit for helping, loving and guiding me to this place. Also thanks went to my parents who were still right by my side with all their love for me. Then there were our other three Ministers who left very large footprints for me to follow that I was grateful for and all of my church family that helped make this an easier journey.

Next I thanked my family, my brother, husband and four kids who were all present, for their support and love for me for who I am and who I was becoming. Most of all I admitted my huge gratitude to Benjamin for turning my whole world upside down so I could see things differently and gain new perspective on life. And last but not least I thanked myself. I was and am very pleased with how my life changed so much for the better and I could not have done it without my inner strength.

There is still, and will always be, ongoing learning and further connecting to Spirit and knowing this, makes me stronger all the time. It was a wonderful day for me and my family and it will be remembered for years to come.

Shortly after, for some reason the parent support group stopped meeting. We just couldn't seem to get together all at the same time, but I have to trust that everything is as it should be.

CHAPTER EIGHTEEN

A special message from Benjamin...

On September 12th 2010 I did a "Moment with Spirit" at our church. That is when someone from the congregation comes up and speaks for five to ten minutes about when or how Spirit has noticeably come to them. I chose that day because it was the day before Benjamin's nineteenth anniversary.

I spoke about writing this book, how much it has helped me, and how hard it has been. What has been hard is not just going back in time to access the memories; it's the emotions that go along with it. It has been less intense through memory than the actual experience, but difficult never the less. I knew I had to go back in my memories to get this information and I am glad I did. I have been guided the whole way.

As we have quite a few people at church that have lost a child, I was hoping to reach their hearts. After the service was over I had a few people come tell me I had done just that. They said some very beautiful things about me and how far I've come, that is always nice to hear, but sometimes I don't feel worthy that I have made the progress that I have. I still have 'The Joy Issue' as I now call it and I don't seem to be progressing as quickly as I would like to in that area.

On my way home I was driving alone in my car and I received a message from Ben. He said "Mom, there will be a part two of the book. I will give you my side of the whole story." Then he was gone. I didn't see him or hear him with my ears; it was just a kind of knowing or maybe an impression in my mind via my heart, because that is where I felt it.

I was elated at such an idea. I'd never read a book like that before. I remember in the beginning Ben said he would be my co-author, but I thought that just meant he would be with me through the process, helping and guiding me.

I knew I would have to do lots of meditating and quiet time for this and I was feeling honoured and excited that I had been given such an incredible opportunity. When I got home I told my husband my message from Ben. He was also excited for me and thought it was a wonderful and unique addition to the book. I told my friend and fellow Minister. She said to me that she felt Ben was going to come through me, but did not know how that was going to happen.

Later that evening I phoned my little brother. I wanted to see what he thought of the new turn of events in my book venture. To be honest with you I began to doubt myself and my ability to do this when I was telling my brother. It did not have anything to do with what I thought my brother was going to say about it, I just began to doubt. After I told him about the message and his response being similar to my husband's, I said that I felt I already knew a lot about near death experience and the like. I have been reading all kinds of books on that subject for over eighteen years and it would be hard for me to know the authenticity of what Ben was giving me as opposed to what I have read. I wondered how I was going to get this information from Ben and write it down exactly as it was given, without my head getting in the way.

I have to say I was feeling a little intimidated and fearful of the second part of the book. My brother said I had to just trust in Ben's ability and believe in myself, by stepping aside from my ego. Sounded good to me, but I wish that's all it took for me to just fly at it, but my doubts were bigger and I needed to deal with them. After thinking about it longer I decided not to tell you, the reader, so if it did not work out, then there would not be a problem.

Sometime later I was telling my husband that I was feeling some doubts and didn't know what Ben could possibly tell me. Then I heard Ben say "You have no idea mom, what I am doing now!" Then I became more confident.

I actually had to let it go and take a break from writing for a while as I had three boys going back to school and needing my care and attention. It was September 2010 and the boys were going into grades eleven, nine and four.

CHAPTER NINETEEN

The opportunity to learn some more....

At the end of September I was helping a lady from our church pack her house for a big move. The first day that I went to help her I had to take my youngest son which was fine with everyone including him. The lady gave my son a beautiful book about fairies. When we were done and about to leave I told him to take the book and wait for me in the car.

As I was going out the door the lady gently pulled me back and said "I have just been given a message from Spirit, do you mind if I share it with you?"

"That would be fine. I would like that." I said, knowing she got messages on occasion. She then asked me if the boy I lost was being held up on a pedestal by me. I told her I didn't believe so.

She continued, "I was shown your boy there, the one in the car saying to you, "Mom I am right here can you not see me?" I'm being told you need to look at this Olivia" Then she said "You may need to think about the message and what it means to you." We hugged good bye and I told her I would see her the following day.

Well, I didn't really know what to think about what she said. I don't feel I put Ben on a pedestal, I do not have a shrine of him, I don't go crying to his grave all the time and I don't feel that I talk about him all the time either as I have a family to raise and am quite busy with them. When someone reminds me of something Ben said or did, then I say something, but I don't think I overdo it, I don't believe everything I read or hear, instead I like to take it all in and see what my heart says is the truth for me.

As for my youngest, he is the type of child that does require a lot of attention. He was only nine years old at the time and I gave him as much attention as I could. As for the "Pedestal thing" I just kind of fluffed that off and carried on with my day.

Our small town nearby, was experiencing heavy sadness. A nineteen-year-old boy was accidently hit and killed by a train; a homeless man was found dead in the park; and one of the ladies from our church lost her only son aged twenty-three.

Then our oldest son told me one of his class mates had committed suicide! All of this happened in one week. Our son was upset. It was a little too close to home and his first experience with this kind of thing. He didn't know the boy very well, but it not only affected the whole school, it seemed to have affected our whole town. The boy was a nice kid, came from a good home and had good grades. It was so hard for the kids at school to wrap their brains around the "Why?"

Our son slipped into a depression about the whole situation. Added to the confusion of puberty, it became a very hard time for him. Being his mother and a highly sensitive person I found myself slipping into a bit of a depression myself. I wanted to make our son feel better, but there was nothing I could do. He

117

is not the talkative kind so I couldn't even be a good listener for him. That only made it harder for both of us.

One Tuesday evening at our church meditation circle I received a message from Ben that one of his brothers was having some trouble and I was not to fluff it off. It was important that I investigate and do what I could do. I wished I got a little more information, because I didn't know which boy or what the problem was. My first thought was that it was my youngest that was having trouble with a bully at school in grade four. I went to the school and dealt with it to the best of my ability and all seemed to be well.

I then noticed that the oldest one was not coming out of his depression. He seemed to be so sad about everything around him. I had a talk with his girlfriend who was very concerned about him. I tried to talk to him, but he has always been so quiet and reserved, I felt like I was talking to a brick wall. I got him some good vitamins and started sneaking some saffron into his meals. Saffron is said to lift the serotonin levels in the brain. I could only hope and pray that it would at least help him a bit for now, until we could figure out our next step.

He then asked me if I could make him a doctor's appointment for some pain he was having in his back. He was not quite sixteen and had shot up to almost six feet tall in a very short period. I went to see the doctor first to tell him what was going on. I have a very good rapport with our doctor after knowing him for twenty years. After I explained he said he would do some counselling with my son and help him in any way he could. I felt a little bit of comfort in that. It went well with the doctor, who adores our son, but our son was still upset. I know from my own experiences that things like this don't usually just go away on their own and with him not communicating; I had to just ride it out for now.

One day my husband expressed that he was a little concerned about his best friend who was not answering his house phone or his cell and his wife was away. I was telling him that it wouldn't hurt for us to take the forty minute drive to check up on him, when our phone rang. It was the high school counsellor asking if we could come to the school, she needed to talk to us. So we figured we could go see his friend as well.

I was still struggling with all the deaths in town and our son's depression and I was feeling a bit sick to my stomach. On the way into town I told my husband that I was scared that the counsellor was going to tell us something had happened to our son. My husband reminded me that the high school counsellor is a friend of ours and a church member and that I shouldn't worry. I have to admit I have an overactive imagination, which coupled with the sadness I was experiencing, was making me upset and scared.

As we drove into town the air was so thick with sadness that you could have cut it with a butter knife. There had also been two more suicides in the last month, not school related.

My stomach was getting worse and it did not help while we were walking into the school that, two ambulances went by with their sirens on. The hospital is only a block from the school. The fear was really getting a hold of me.

We entered the counsellor's office, she told us to sit down. I had to move a box of Kleenex from the chair to sit and was glad I had just put it on my lap. When she told us that she called us in on a church matter, I lost it. I cried so hard, with relief. I didn't seem to have any control over what was happening to me. When she asked me what was wrong I could not even

speak, so my husband told her what I had said to him in the
car. I cried for a good long time, the energy in the school was
so sad and it was heartbreaking. My friend said she wished she
had told me on the phone why she wanted us to come in and
added that she was sorry she hadn't.

We left there and went to check on my husband's friend and
thank God he was ok, just not wanting to answer the phone. I
was thinking that I got caught up in all of this for some reason
and I was glad it was not our son or our friend. I was a little
puzzled about my outburst though. Later I discovered that it is
called "cellular memory."

When we were at the school, the counsellor told me that
the boy that took his own life was showing some signs and that
it hadn't just happened out of the blue. So on our way home I
said to my husband that after school I was going to tell our son
that there was some signs from that boy, so he could maybe
understand the whole thing better and make it a little easier
on him.

When he got home I asked him to come outside so I could
talk to him alone. I told him about the boy's signs and of his
plans. Our son didn't say anything, I started crying again and
told him that I didn't know that if there was anything going on
with him, if he would come and talk to me about it. He again
didn't say a word. I said through my waterfall of tears, which
he had never seen me like that before, "I love you so much and
I just wanted to let you know that." No words from him, so I
stood up to give him a huge hug. The way he hugged me back
was so tight, loving and safe, I then realized no words were
necessary.

He went in the house and I stayed and balled my eyes out.
I was wondering if that awesome hug he gave me was an "I

love you so much too" hug or was it a "good-bye" hug. My emotions were overriding me, I had not cried like this since Ben passed. I knew the whole situation was bringing up some suppressed grief, but knowing that did not make it any easier.

I received a couple more phone calls from his girlfriend not knowing what to do for him. I reassured her that everything would be okay, but I was not sure if I believed that myself.

The following Sunday it was my turn to do the service, as there are four Ministers we each took the service once a month. I was still beside myself, but I had stopped crying for now. Before I went into the church I asked Spirit to please guide me through this to do a wonderful job and that was granted thankfully.

After church I was talking to my dear friend, one of the Ministers, and telling her of my woes of the last two to three weeks. She asked me very gently "Do you think you hold Benjamin on a pedestal?"

I snapped at her, "No I don't!" But then admitted what the lady had said to me about a month before that.

Her reply to that was "Okay you don't, but what do you think your boy thinks about that?" I had never thought of it that way before and that gave me a much different view on the whole situation. I had not thought it could affect my son or anyone else for that matter. So I thanked her and went on my way with something new to think about and consider.

I have friends that are a couple, who do a special kind of alternative healing, where during meditation, their higher self, talks to the higher self of the person they are doing the healing on. I was taught this method some years ago so I trust the authenticity of this kind of healing. I asked them if they could do a healing on my son. They both replied with a "Yes."

The next day I went to see them and the male friend said that our son was struggling with lack of self- love and some earlier abandonment issue. I feel that a high percentage of teens going through puberty and high school have low self-esteem. His abandonment issue, I'm sure, had to do with his father leaving at the age of eight. I was wide open to give our son answers to any questions or help him in any way I could, if he would only ask me. I was empathetic to him, about his dad leaving, and I understood it could be the reason for some of his grief.

My female friend said she had a conversation with our son's higher-self and this is what she told me, "Every time you talk about your family you include the boy you lost. It is hurting your older son; he feels that he would get more attention if he were in the same place as Ben". She added "I am only giving you what I got."

Wow, what do I do? On my way home all I could do was cry, again. I was so confused, Ben was my son too. I have always said "We can sometimes get wonderful gifts in really crappy wrapping paper." This was one of those times.

When my husband got home I asked him if he felt I talked about Ben too much. He said very quietly "Not really." That reply was a little suspicious the way he said it, but I left it alone. I needed to call my little brother who knew better than anyone what I had been through. When he got on the phone I said hi then "Do you think I put Ben on a pedestal?"

In a clear voice he said "Yes! You do and you always have."

"Oh my God! What the hell am I supposed to do? All four of them are my sons. I'm writing this book about Ben. What am I to do, stop writing and just throw the book away?

I don't know what to do or how to handle this." I yelled back at my brother.

His answers to my questions were "You need to separate them. I will tell you what I feel, if you want to hear it."

"Okay, because I am so stuck right now. I don't want to hurt my boys anymore."

"I feel your oldest boy thinks he is in competition with Ben, with someone that cannot do anything wrong, an Angel." I thanked my brother and got off the phone.

That was it, now I got it. That is what I needed to hear. Of course I never thought of it that way and I think that's what my friend was saying to me after church that day, in a roundabout way.

Well, I cried most of that night. I knew my brother was right, but I had no idea what to do about it. I thought I was doing all the right things for Ben, my other children and myself. I was in so much pain and I felt so alone. This aloneness I was feeling, I discovered later, was another crappy wrapped gift because it took me deeper inside where I needed to go. I was also feeling some anger towards myself for messing up with my older son, however I didn't take that too far as I didn't know what I was doing. Now I felt like I had to say good bye to Ben all over again and it really hurt.

In bed I cried some more and I prayed for help, "What do I do or what do I stop doing and how?" Then I was shown a kind of block in my path. The block was not Ben it was me who put it there and it was blocking my joy. Spirit showed me for just a split second my future if I chose to remove that block. They showed me joy in my marriage, with my children and grandchildren to come, as well as all my relationships. It was beautiful!

123

"But, what about Benjamin?" I cried. I was told I didn't have to forget about Ben and I could always hold him in my heart and I would always remember him, but not to let that block the boys' growth and opportunity to be joyful. That sounded familiar to me. I knew that I was never really alone, I knew I had Guides and Angels with me always, but had I not felt alone at the time I may not have gotten the lesson in that moment. I finally fell asleep in the wee hours of the morning.

I felt a lot better the next morning and I had stopped crying. I hoped that all that pain last night had removed that block from my path, but only time would tell.

A couple of days later our youngest came in my room and looked up at the picture of Ben that I had put together for Christmas, so many years ago. He looked at me with teary eyes and said "I really wish I would have met Ben, mom."

I said "You did before you came here and you will again when you leave." He was good with that, said okay and hopped out of my room wearing a contented smile. I was thinking to myself that my sons are all so different. I can't talk about Ben with one of them, one needs me to, and the boy in the middle could hear about Ben or not.

I knew it was hard to raise kids, but after I lost Ben I had no idea how much harder it would make raising future children. I'm sure I would not have found all of this out had I not gone through this recent experience with our older boy, which I now am truly grateful for. As parents we have to be so careful, but we also have to be ourselves and teach our kids that, that's okay.

One day I had the opportunity to talk to our second oldest boy, who is much more into communication, due to his personality. I was able to tell him everything I had just gone through and he was an awesome listener. I asked if he thought I held Ben on a pedestal according to his perception. He said that sometimes it felt that way, but the thing he had noticed was that I had never said anything about Ben doing anything wrong or bad. Feeling a bit defensive I told of the time Ben smoked a cigarette butt and punched his sister really hard in the face. Then I told him that Ben only made it to five years old and didn't have a lot of time to do anything bad. I also added that none of them had done anything bad or wrong by that age either, not even tried to smoke a cigarette butt. He laughed.

He told me he'd be glad to tell me privately if I had gone overboard about Ben. I was truly grateful to have an honest scale to go by now.

CHAPTER TWENTY

Conclusion to part one....

I was still struggling with things, but doing my best to feel good about myself, who I am, who I was becoming and even who I used to be. Also I was working on how to separate things that needed to be separated and keep together the things that needed keeping together, kind of like the serenity prayer, which I had been reciting a lot as well.

Our daughter and her man came for Thanksgiving in mid-October and again it was a wonderful visit. It is my favourite time when all the kids are together, because that's when I feel Ben's presence the most. They all get along so well together. That is joy for me.

Our daughter has a full time job now that keeps her very busy. She still has some struggles, but looks at them differently now. We did have a great visit, but then they had to go and right away I felt a little down, and I was still feeling upset about our oldest son's depression.

My birthday was coming up and I was not far from having the birthday blues. I had a friend come over the night before to see me and she brought me a lovely card and some beautiful flowers that were uplifting.

I have been friends with her for about six years. She owns a daycare and my three boys were her first kids when she opened up. She is such a lovely lady and we became close instantly, kindred Spirits would be my guess. She is married to the fellow that was on the dirt bike with Ben.

When she came over the night before my birthday she said she had been talking to her husband one day recently about how he felt about Ben and the accident. He said to her that he wondered if I as Ben's mother could ever forgive him. This statement lightened my heavy mood so quickly, knowing that I may have an opportunity to talk to him after nineteen years.

I had written countless letters to him over the years to let him know that he was forgiven, but could not ever send them for one reason or another and wondered if I would ever have the opportunity to sit down and talk to him about it. I tried to set up a meeting with him and it just didn't work out, yet. I then realized I needed to give this over to Spirit and allow that intervention to take over in Divine timing, and that I would be guided and I just needed to be patient.

There was a couple in our church who lost their son in a car accident. They have two young adult boys so I asked them if they could give me some insight on the whole male puberty thing and their experiences with their boys. They were helpful to a point, but as we all know everyone is so different. I was just trying to be an informed and understanding parent when it came to the subject of puberty, considering I had two more boys to go.

A new lady joined our church; she was friends with the couple I just mentioned. She lost one of her two sons years ago when he was two and a half years old. He choked on a peanut, something about that just seems to be so sad to me. I had a nice chat with her after church and she told me something that I found very strange. She said that she, her ex-husband, the other couple from church and a third couple use to hang out together. Their husbands all worked at the same place, they all had boys and spent a lot of time together. What she said that I found strange was, after her boy passed they were all very helpful, then years later the other couple lost their boy in the car accident and again everyone was helpful, but stranger yet was that the third couple were the parents of the young boy from the school who committed suicide just months ago.

All I could think was that God worked in mysterious ways and we form certain bonds with certain people, for reasons we may never know, but there is a grand plan. And sometimes we do get the gift of knowing.

Suddenly one day I was guided to go by my friend's place, the one whose husband was with Ben. He was out in the driveway shovelling snow. I was guided to stop and asked him if we could take a little time and have a talk. He was willing. I had spoken to him over the years as this is a small place, but it was always just a casual "Hi, how are you doing?" kind of conversation.

It was hard to start out the conversation, but we did speak for about forty minutes and it was very good for me. I sure hoped that it made him feel somewhat better.

I told him there had been a couple of things that kept me going over the years, one of them being that I knew Ben was with me a lot of the time and I could even feel him and that this was helpful and gave me strength. The other was that I now knew that it was Ben's time or it would not have happened. He disagreed on the second one due to the way he was raised. He said "Children are like Angels and they should not die." I couldn't really argue that with him or I should say I wouldn't. He had every right to his own beliefs and I was not there to change them, only to share with him what had worked for me.

I said to him "If you need to hear this, I totally and completely forgive you, but I feel there is nothing to forgive you for, because you did not do anything wrong. It was all as it should be." There definitely were some tears from both of us, but we parted with a huge hug. When I left I thought of so many other things I wanted to or wished I had said, but I was truly grateful for that long awaited opportunity, and felt confident that we may get more opportunities down the road and I felt good about the whole thing.

I did some praying for him and myself and was feeling better, better than I had in months. I knew I was now, back on track and could start writing again, it had been quite some time since I had written. After the situation with our older son I wasn't sure that I should even be writing this book, but luckily I was reminded that I was told by Angels to write it in the first place. I had that much faith to know they would not lead me down a path that would harm anyone or that did not have a purpose.

My husband took a working trip in December to visit our daughter and her man. He stayed for about three weeks and thoroughly enjoyed himself and the time spent getting to know his new daughter. Then they all showed up for an absolutely wonderful Christmas. They asked me at that time if I would do the honours of performing their wedding for them in about a year or so. I was the one that felt honoured.

Our older son seemed to be doing much better. He turned sixteen two days after Christmas. He is such an incredible soul and I love him more than I can say. I am truly grateful for all those who have helped us get through this process.

As for Part Two of this book, I have done a lot of reading and meditation on communicating with Spirit and our loved ones on the other side and am feeling much more confident. I just need to fully trust Ben and believe in myself and everything will flow perfectly together as my Angels have by guiding me to do.

Recently I read a fascinating book called "The Healing Code" which has information on cellular memories. Knowing myself, the way I do, I learn much better with the use of metaphors. At that time, we were getting the boys to walk the one kilometre up the mountain after school; since the younger one was only ten I was walking down to get him. It was great exercise for all of us and a nice time for my youngest and I to talk. After church one Sunday we saw some neighbours of ours while we were in town, who live by the boys' bus stop. They asked us if we were aware that there was a cougar in the neighbourhood. We said no, we hadn't heard. I am terrified of cougars; they are so sneaky and unpredictable. We have bears around, but you can clap your hands loudly and they will usually run away, not cougars though.

It was Monday and I was talking to my friend on the phone, my friend that has been by my side all these years, about the cougar. She too has kids and lives out in the bush. The bus arrives at 3:30 pm with our youngest and then again at 4:45 pm with the other two. My friend said "You better get going; it's 3:29 pm." I was surprised and a little freaked that I wasn't paying attention to the time, especially under the circumstances. I said bye and flew out the door, I made it to the stop at 3:31 pm. There was no bus yet, which is quite common, it can come anywhere between 3:25 pm and 3:35 pm.

I was starting to go into a slight panic, when the clock in the car said 3:42 pm. My breathing started to get shallow and my heart rate went up, when it was 3:45 pm I got worse. I started looking around out my window for his back pack and drag marks. I was saying to myself not to get upset and let my imagination get hold of me. Then came 3:48 pm and I wondered if he had maybe hid in the ditch on my way down, and if so I would wait till 3:50 pm then have to go home and check. The problem with that was I could not move, my body wouldn't let me. I had now become temporarily paralyzed and surely could not leave the bus stop. What if the bus came? You have to understand I was now terrified with sweaty palms and very shallow and quick breathing. The bus pulled up at 3:51pm and my beautiful boy hopped off and jumped in the car no worse for wear. He told me that there was a tree down on the road and they had to take a detour.

When my husband got home ten minutes later I was a wreck. He asked me what was wrong and I told him. He was so empathetic, he hugged me tightly and said "I'm so sorry you had to go through that."

The next day I was reading that book the "Healing Code", I read about when our bodies kick into fight or flight because of cellular memory, and that quite often the memory can be unconscious and we have no idea where it came from. The reason why I tell you this is because the panic due to the late bus was about losing Ben and the unconscious going into fight or flight because my body does not want to go through anything like that again. It was another huge lesson for me and I didn't like it, but these are the kind of things we can go through for the rest of our lives after having gone through a past tragedy. I was thankful that the book I was reading was exactly the information I needed at the time.

Our daughter is doing awesome on her journey and I could not have been more pleased. The boys are growing up to be such nice young men and I am so proud of all my children. Their respect, support and love have made it easier for me to keep breathing. And my new husband is definitely a keeper. I appreciate his strength and, am grateful for the admiration he has for me. I have been extremely blessed.

As I finish part one and make sure it is all ready to go to the publishing company it is now March 2011. My beautiful daughter and her ex-man have had a sad break-up and will now be going their own ways. I am sending both of them lots of loving and healing Angels. At the conclusion of part one the children were aged twenty-seven, seventeen, fifteen and eleven years. If any of you are curious about their dad, my ex-husband, we never did hear another word from him since September 2006; I continue to send him healing love. Unfortunately our special cat, that stuck it out with me, went home to be with Ben just a couple of months before she turned twenty years old.

I have to say that I have had an emotionally hard time writing this book, but if I can touch just one other person's heart that has lost a beloved child and help them feel that their child is still close to them it will have all been worth it.

I am content now in knowing where my son is. I believe all the questions I had so many years ago have been answered and I feel the truth of those answers in my heart and I am truly grateful for that. A lot of healing has been achieved through writing this book for me.

I am starting to look forward to Part Two of this book. The opportunity to write with Benjamin is the most incredible gift I could ever receive.

PART TWO

Benjamin tells his story.... Questions and Answers....

Introduction

To Part Two

This part of the book was difficult for me in the beginning, because I had a hard time believing in myself and trusting the process of channelling. The more I tried the better it got and the more comfortable I got. Benjamin made it easy for me and I appreciate that so much. Thank you, Ben for all your help, patience and the few surprises along the way.

I do give messages from people's deceased loved ones at church all the time and Angel card readings, but this to me was different. The messages at church are quick and to the point for that person and I do not need to understand the messages as they are not for me, they only go through me.

There is Clairvoyance, which is clear seeing. When someone picks up on a presence from the other side and sees them with their minds eye.

Then, there is Clairaudience, which is clear hearing, when someone hears with their inner ear the voices from beyond.

Clairsentience is clear feeling. If someone has had a heart attack and passed they may give the feeling of pain in the heart or chest area.

And Claircognance, this is when you have a clear knowing, but not know how you would know that information.

Benjamin told me to have a clipboard, paper and a special pen; he let me know which pen. He asked me to do this part of the connecting with him in my office away from the phones and any disturbances and he said he really loved the energy in there. I lit a small candle and put a C.D. on with sounds of rain and mellow piano music, very peaceful and serene. When I was ready and I felt comfortable, I began.

I was first told to write a list of questions I wanted answered. I have a picture of Ben that I put in his obituary and I pulled it out each time, I greeted him with a kiss and told him I was ready to begin. I said a quick prayer of gratitude to Ben and the Angels, wrote the first question down, then sat patiently (As patiently as I could under the circumstances) until I was moved to start writing. Whatever came to my mind I just wrote it down on the paper. Some of the things I wrote, I've known about and some I had not. We only did this for an hour to two at a time, because of the energy we both needed. Benjamin's words have not been edited or altered, except for punctuation and spelling, because I felt it was important to give you exactly what I was given.

My husband and I do this trance work. I put him in a trance, and then he speaks to the "Client's" higher-self and asks for permission to do what is called a scan of the body and aura. Like a medical intuitive, but in a deep trance. I thought one night as I was falling asleep if there was any way I could hypnotize my husband and see if he could talk with or for Ben from his trance state. The next morning I asked him how he felt about doing that and he said "As long as it is okay with Benjamin." The last three questions are asked this way, with a little surprise for me.

Please have an open mind and heart for this part of the book, and take what you like and leave the rest. However, if something makes you feel uncomfortable please just skip over it or leave it for now, but here is what I got.

I am here in my office with an open heart to communicate with my son and favourite Angel Benjamin. As requested by him, to allow him to come through me (I am so honoured) to relate his story since he passed in September 1991.

_ How would you like to start off Ben?

"Hi mom, I guess we will just get started. Remember when I watched HOME ALONE the movie and how much I laughed? But do you also remember when I was sad a while later and I yelled at you that I wanted to wake up at home alone and didn't want any of you there?"

_Yes, I sure do remember.

"It was then that I knew I was going 'Home'. You were not supposed to understand that sign at the time, so please don't be hard on yourself for not getting it, there was nothing you could have done anyway."

"It was my time and I know you know that now and have done for quite some time."

"When we were driving home from town that afternoon on the thirteenth of September, when you said I was somewhere far away, I want to confirm that for you. I was, part of me, my soul I guess was checking out, the other side, the Spirit realm, before I really left. I was not conscious of what was happening so it wasn't something I could tell you about at the time, I hope you understand that mom."

"I went 'Home' because it was my time and we as a family had contracted that before we all came to the earth plain. I did not leave because it wasn't

137

good with you guys, this is very important that you understand mom. I loved my life, my family and my bike!"

_Ben can you please tell me or show me what happened at the accident site?

"I want you to know mom, I was having the time of my life on the bike ride, as I always did, and it was a certain kind of freedom and so much fun for me."

"We turned off the main road onto the logging road and that is when I began to feel the bright light. We were not going very fast, I wanted him to go faster. The last thing I remember was when he craned his neck around to look right at my face and I smiled to let him know how much fun I was having and he smiled back. Then everything went black ...., but only for a moment. Mom I passed instantly, but I stayed to help him find my body after I went flying through the air. Right away I felt all kinds of Angels there and it was so pretty, the lights and the feeling of pure love. His Angels were there too, to help him, but he could not hear them or me. I was trying to pull on his ears so he could hear me, but he was very scared and went into shock right away. At that time I felt a gentle pull to go into the brighter part of the light, but I wanted to stay a bit longer, until you came."

"When you bent down to X and O me, I slipped in between you and my body. You X and Oed my soul and I felt all the love you had for me, and then I started to go 'Home'."

_ **You may refer back to Chapter Two in part one of the book as a reminder of this statement. What was that like for you Ben?**

"I was surrounded by Angels; everywhere, I was not scared at all, mom. I didn't recognize any of them at first. I only knew that they knew me and they were all full to the brim with unconditional love for me. I looked back and you were still bent over me, but the whole scene was getting smaller and smaller. I yelled to you how much I love you, dad and my sister, but you could not hear me."

"Rainbows over the clouds! I was flying with the Angels right through the rainbow clouds, up and up till we came to the land of rainbows. Everything was beautiful bright rainbows in forms of buildings, trees, water and land. I began to recognize the Angels I was with; I knew them before I came to you. My grandma was the first one that I recognized and I remembered her from when I was about one week old just after I was born when we were still in the hospital. She helped me stay with you."

_ **What did that feel like for you?**

"It felt beautiful, yet familiar. It was like the ultimate of pure love, compassion and joy."

"What happened next was so cool, a magic rainbow school bus came and picked me up. Remember how badly I wanted to ride the school bus like my sister, but I was just too young? Then I started recognizing all the energies I was meeting up with. We drove on

139

the rainbow road, I'm not sure if the bus was driving or the road was moving."

"I have been told that I cannot tell you everything, you have to wait for your time to come home, and then you will remember it all. One thing I can tell you is that I was able to come back and say good-bye to you that night.

You were not dreaming. I was really and truly there, when you held my face and kissed me all over. You fell asleep before I left and I put my teddy bear, "Beary", in your arms. When you woke up he was still there."

"All the meditations, dreams and messages you have had from me have been a direct link with me, just like right now. I have been told that you will only develop this gift more and more so that you can share it with others who need to know that their loved ones are not dead. You need to work on trusting and believing in yourself more than anything. It is also important for you to doubt as well, it keeps you searching for more and you are in a human body still and humans act like humans."

"I am so proud of my sister and all she has learned. She is so beautiful, but the beauty I see is much different then what you can see. She still has a hidden light that will be shining on the world and all whom she touches, when she's ready. My brothers are so awesome mom. I know you are doing the best you can with them, but you still need to trust more in yourself, that you are doing a good job. Believe in *them as individuals, that their higher selves will bring them all that they need."*

"I see an incredible vibration coming from your home. That is what we see from our vantage point, is vibration. There is a lot of love emulating from that house, know that, and just trust it. None of you will ever be given more than you can handle, this is true."

_What have you been doing on the other side?

"I went to school for a long time to learn on a Spiritual level. I learned about the contracts we make and fulfill on earth and other places too.

I know that you have a hard time with the OTHER places mom, but you asked the question and I can only answer with the truth."

_ The other places Ben is referring to are other planets and in the past I have had a hard time believing in such a thing. Now I have more of an open mind.

Benjamin speaks of lifetime after lifetime in some areas, so I thought I better let the reader know the difference between reincarnations: The rebirth of a soul in a new body. Immortality: living forever; never dying. Ben is referring to reincarnation not immortality.

"A part of everyone's soul stays on the other side or Heaven as some would prefer to call it, always, to guide and monitor our earthly lives. This is our higher self. Our souls as a whole are very powerful, too powerful to be contained in one human body at one time. You do understand this I know."

"I am back on the earth plain now, but I will leave that where it is. All you need to know is that when, like now, I am with you it is the part of me that stays here, my higher self."

"For the longest time I watched you, dad and my sister. It was hard for me in the beginning because you were all so heartbroken. One of the things I learned in my classes here is that it is all exactly the way it is meant to be. I learned quickly that when I was watching you guys you were with me, the part of you that stays here always, your higher selves. I felt great comfort in that."

"I want you to know I was with my sister when she had her bad car accident. I and many, many Angels made sure that she would be okay. She was not on the "Times up List" so to speak. I was also with you when you had your car accident. Just to let you know firsthand, you have some very powerful Angels and an incredible team here that works with you all the time. Please know this mom."

"I know you felt me all three times, but I'll tell you anyway. I was right beside you on your right-hand side when you brought all three of my brothers into your world. It was beautiful and so are they, they have very special souls, and you have been so blessed, so blessed with all five of us. I remember when we sat together on this side and picked you to be our earthly mother this time. You are aware that we are your teachers I know, but I want to tell you that you have been a willing and open student. I know some times it

is hard for you, but it is only because of your human
shell, your soul completely understands."

**_ Ben if you are able, can you tell me how your dad is
doing?**

"In an earthly opinion he is not doing well, but
he is doing exactly what he signed up to do. Dad's
biggest lesson this time is to love himself for whom he
is in every moment, and he struggles with this a lot, as
most humans do. He is right where he is supposed to
be as all of you are. Mom all the love, forgiveness and
healing Angels you have sent to dad are all working
and I personally thank you for doing that. It has
helped you in your healing process as well."

"I hang out with grandma and grandpa a lot and
they want me to tell you that they could not be more
pleased with your Spiritual advancements. They say
you have done them proud, yep that's right mom,
grandpa said proud".

**_ My dad did not like the word proud when he was here,
I guess he sees it differently now.**

"Mom your parents love you so much and are still
and always will be very connected to you."

"Mom what do you think about that wonderful
man we sent to you in late 2006? We know that you
have struggled with worthiness for having such a man
like that in your life after all this time, but you seem
to be slowly getting it. Grandpa is asking if you have
noticed the similarities in him and your man."

_ **My new husband is way more like my dad than my first husband. He is so patient, loving, kind and trusting.**

"He is so good for you and you for him, you all make a beautiful family."

"Stop worrying about my brother! The oldest of the three, one day he is going to shine his light so brightly you just wait and see. Trust that you have and are doing a good job. No you are doing a great job so stop worrying, and remember that worrying is like paying a debt you may never owe. They, like my sister, all have their own paths. So don't block them, just be as loving and supportive as you can and all the pieces will come together to make an awesome puzzle. Yes, mom it is that simple."

_ **The next three questions were done on September 13TH 2011, Ben's twentieth anniversary. The first question is about a mountain across the lake from where we live. When my husband, boyfriend at the time, showed me his home he said "I have to first show you the pregnant woman." So as curious as I am I said "Okay, what are you talking about, a pregnant women?" Then he pointed to the mountain across the lake from his house, it has a face, long neck, breasts and a big pregnant stomach. I said "That's not just any pregnant woman, that's Mother Earth." She's spectacular and so life like; I fell in love with her right away. I include this description to give you an image for the next question.**

_ Ben from your prospective can you tell me, what the special connection is that I seem to have with the mountain (Mother Earth) across the lake?

"The word mother is the connection! Your mother, you and the earth's mother all hold that same kind of energy. You feel strength, compassion, nurturing and patience. You receive that energy every time you look at it. No one else gets that energy to the degree that you do, it's what pulled you to where you are and now live. Others see its beauty maybe even feel it, but not to the extent that you do."

"One day you will be able to literally see that incredible energy emulating off the mountain, coming across the lake and into your body, and you will soon be able to receive messages from that grand mountain that you call Mother Earth. You do not need to go hiking on her; you are exactly in the perfect position to receive, when you are clearly ready. These messages will be from your higher self, your mother, my grandma, and the Earth mother. Be patient, trust and believe in yourself."

_ Ben, lately I have been getting the same messages from books that I read, the internet and radio interviews, that we as humans are so loved from the other side, if only we knew. We are so loved for who we are right now no matter what. Is there anything you can tell me about this?

"If all humans knew how much unconditional love there was from here, there would be no wars, hatred, or negativity. That's what is wrong on the

earth plain. That is where judgement is. There is none
of that here, because it serves no purpose. I suppose
it serves some purpose there, but it's a very hard way
to learn."

"Your loved ones, guides and Angels see you,
all of you for who you truly are, in pure perfection,
pure light and pure love. I'm wondering if it's just a
little too much for the human mind to take, but know
this mom, it is a fact. There is not one human that is
so bad, that they are not seen with this pure love or
receive it, not any person, animal or plant, not even
plants that are poison."

"If you could only see what we see from here,
it would fix everything I'm sure, but that's not the
plan. If people could connect more often with their
higher-selves, the part that stays here, they would get
beautiful glimpses of this pure loving wonder."

_ **Are you indeed here with us when we are all together
as a family, because my husband and I both swear we
saw you the last time your sister was here?**

"Of course, do you think I would miss an
opportunity to be with all of you at the same time? It
does not take me a long time to travel from my sister's
place to yours, but it is a perfect situation when you
are all together. I know that you have noticed this for
a long time that is why I recently tried to validate my
presence to both of you. I was running around the
house in glee that day, and quite surprised everybody
did not see me. Do not be afraid to ask my brothers
and sister if they see, feel or sense me there. I know my

146

sister does, but she still does not trust or believe in her
own abilities yet to not explain it away to something
earthly."

**_ Can you tell me more about your journey home, as I
write today on your twentieth anniversary?**

*"The love from the other side we just spoke about
is there right away. It is tangible, so much so I started
to cry actually, because it is so pure, perfect and loving,
this energy."*

*"It does not hurt, the more you trust the less pain
you feel. The rainbows are magnificent! I have heard
you say that you feel rainbows are a glimpse of the
beauty and unconditional love from the other side.
That is so true. It is like Spirit opens up a bit of the
sky to show you what home looks like. This is my
soul's perception, not all others see it this way."*

*"Earthly life is a personal journey of soul growth,
we take the experiences we learned on the earth and
other places back home to view them without judgement
or pain. Then and only then do we truly learn and
understand who we really are and why. I don't really
view earth as a school, it to me is more of a place you
go to collect the experiences and feelings, then bring
them back home and learn here why they happened.
I don't believe you can learn fully with all that self-
judgement never mind the negative judgements from
others. We don't have that here, so it is much easier
to understand and accept this way."*

*"This we do not do alone, all others that we
have touched or hurt in this lifetime are here with us*

and are all loving without judgement. We sit around tables and talk about what we did or did not do in that particular lifetime, but sometimes we need to go back a couple or several lifetimes.

What I mean by that is, if I am talking to you, that part of you that stays here, about what it was like for you to lose a son, I may not fully understand therefore I may need to access a past life where I had lost a child or had a similar experience. You are not angry at me for leaving, because through love it is completely understood that our experiences on earth and other places are for our soul growth. Not only do we have that part of our souls here, we also have our Spirit Guides, Guardian Angels, Ascended Masters and our loved ones. It is like the best party you ever attended."

"When I first arrived here there was a celebration to welcome me home. Your mom, my grandma, brought me to the celebration and to my Angels. That is when I got to see all my loved ones and reunited with them and my true self. After that my Angel took me to other places I needed to go and it was in the other places where I got to be with Guides and Ascended Masters. Sometime after that, I do not know how long, because we don't have time here, not like you guys, I started going to school, SPIRIT SCHOOL, now that is real school!"

"Mom, I know you have read a lot of books on this subject, the books by Dr. Michael Newton explain it quite well, very close to what I perceive."

_ **Can you tell anything that would help me grow and develop my gifts so I can better serve while I am here?**

"You have stuff that you still need to let go of, then you will be more open to learning what can work for you. Not only have you chosen to commit to a life of service, you also signed up for it before you went to the earth. You need to be more patient and not in such a hurry. Everything will fall into place as it does. Maybe you could try to go with the flow more, knowing everything happens for a reason is helpful. Stop pushing against things so much."

"Self-forgiveness is where it is at! We both know you have done a lot and have come a long way, but sometimes you are so hard on yourself. When you are hard on yourself it pushes you back every time. And then that causes you more grief. I know it is hard, because I can see that kind of energy coming from humans when they do this to themselves; it is worse what people do to themselves then what others do to them or what they do to others, from what we see."

"When you truly forgive yourself you will advance so much quicker. It is so much harder for mothers, as they have to be responsible and let go at the same time. It is hard to know what to do, when to do it and when to let go and trust. You sometimes have to do both and it has to be at the right time, and that can be a struggle. Mom, do some more self-forgiveness work and the more you do the easier it will ALL get. Everything will get better and work out and you know this, you just have to take action and make it work.

You know the saying "When you know better, you do better!" You know better mom, now forgive and let go so you can do better. I know that you are going to do this, because I have the faith in you that you need in yourself."

_ Ben do you know if the veil between the earth plain and the Spirit world is indeed thinning?

"Yes it is. As the earth goes through her major shift, vibrations are raising in the earth and her people. Both animals and humans are learning more and becoming more conscious, as this happens it thins the veil. The veil was set up by humans and their collective unconsciousness many, many years ago. It was a, dis-believe so to speak. People getting mixed up with the power they had and how to use it. They have used their power to benefit themselves on an ego level rather than helping the entire plant and its people on a loving soul level."

"The shift in the earth is natural, but the higher consciousness and people learning to live from their hearts, not their heads, is making the shift's outcome more positive. The shift has happened before in the past, but humans were not able to understand it. This time the changes are more positive for the planet and the people."

"It is about each soul's growth as to how they see the veil, thick or thin. People must have a belief system in their hearts. It does not have to be the same as there are many paths that lead to our same Oneness! You have a belief system in your heart mom that you have

put there through your experiences, not someone else
telling you what to believe. I see you as a very strong
soul to have been able to change that in this lifetime. I
must tell you mom that I still see some doubt in your
heart and it is put there by you as well. It is all part of
your life's lessons. I feel that you need to trust more in
yourself, belief and trust are not the same. Go ahead
and look it up and see for yourself."

"The bigger and more open someone's heart is,
and the more a person lives from their heart, the
thinner the veil, for them."

_ Do you have any suggestions about how to hang on,
during the earth's shift? I and many others find the
vibration to be very high and hard for us to handle.

"You are right, it is hard for everyone. What
you need to hang on to is your soul, the purity, trust
and unconditional love of your soul. Remember you
and everyone on the planet right now were picked to
be there at this time for a reason. You don't have to
know the reason, some of you do though, and it was
contracted by all. It will all work out to be exactly as
it shall, which will be perfect. This is not what you
want to hear mom, I'm sure."

"The vibration is at its highest in the history of
the planet and the best thing you can do is not to fear
it. Fear is heavy, but strong, people need to add to
the lighter and loving energy for a better outcome. It is
hard, but it will be worth it for thousands of years and
millions and millions of people until the next shift,
the better the outcome this time the better for always.

151

All of you there now are the teachers for many more generations to come. You will all make for a better history on our planet earth."

"I have to tell you though that there are a lot of people on the planet right now that do not think they can handle the high vibration and we see it from here. More and more souls are coming here, they are 'checking out' you could say."

_ Why is that Ben?

"As I said they THINK with their human mind that they cannot handle it, but if they felt through their hearts they would know different. So I guess that is what I would suggest to you, is to really make an effort to change over from the head thinking to the heart feeling to see it differently."

"You must remember this has been happening, the shift that is, for years and it is coming to an end soon. What I mean by that is the struggles and hard to handle energies are going to begin to soften and it will become easier. However it is important that people make this change to the heart consciousness now."

_ Can you tell me of a past life that you and I had together and who we were to each other?

"It was in 1706 in Spain. I was your mother and you were a pirate that never returned home from sea. You had a dark side to you at the time that I could not do anything about. I don't know how you passed away, you just never came home. I had heard the ship you were on was coming back, so I made the journey

down to the docks to welcome you home, but you did not get off the ship. I asked a fellow that staggered off the ship if you were coming and he said "Oh, he didn't make it." Then he walked straight to the pub. I didn't follow, I had known in my heart, but I had to check it out anyway."

"I was heartbroken; you were only seventeen years old and my only child. Now, I would be all alone as your father had died of fever many years previous and you were all I had. I lived to be quite old, fragile and alone. We have had many lives together and will continue as we are from the same soul circle."

_ Ben can you please tell me what a 'soul circle' is?

"Well, it is a group of souls that comes together life after life with lessons and purpose for each other. You know how sometimes you look into someone's eyes and they seem familiar, maybe you do not recognize them, but you feel something. The eyes are the window to the soul."

"We set it all up before we go to earth; we do it together and are always lovingly guided as we are on earth."

_ Can you please tell me more about 'soul circles' I find it quite fascinating?

"Yes, soul circles or soul groups are a group of souls that stay together for many lifetimes. Quite often they are family members like mom, brother, aunt or a close friend, but usually they are souls that stick together and are close in each lifetime. That is not to say on some occasions a

soul from another circle will go in a different group for one life time. There will always be a loving purpose and growth for all souls involved in those kinds of situations. You may find in one lifetime, a member of your circle will take your life in some way or commit some heinous crime this time and next time they are a victim. You may call this karma if you like, but it is about experiencing all kinds of different things while on the earth to take to the other side to learn from, for our soul growth."

"Murder here is neither bad nor good, it is not labeled either or. Here it is one of the many lessons that need to be experienced to grow."

"Each soul that signs a contract with you does so out of the unconditional love they have for you. If you wanted to experience in your next lifetime physical pain at another's hand for the purpose of forgiveness, then someone in your soul circle would step forward and say to you something like this, "I will come into your next life and physically hurt you, so you can forgive and we can both grow in that area. I will have to lower my vibration to do so, but I will do it because of the love I have for you and myself as growing souls." Do you understand mom how that works?

There is no bad, evil or negativity, only what humans come up with in their restricted minds."

"Almost everyone that has touched you in this lifetime in a positive or negative way has been of or contracted to your soul circle. I personally like the name soul circle rather than soul group because a circle goes on forever as is my belief of our learning and growing process."

_ Ben, I was going to ask you about forgiveness, but I got a pretty good understanding from your last answer, so thank you. Is there anything else you want to tell me about forgiveness that you didn't say in the last answer?

> *"It is a human thing. There is no need for forgiveness here, because of the complete understanding of the lessons of forgiveness. But where you are it is vitally important that you forgive one another. The most important place to start is within. Self-forgiveness is the hardest to do. I know that I have already told you, that you have some more forgiving to do of yourself and you will. I know you do not like the word stupid, but that is the only human word I can come up with right now. Not forgiving yourself is just plain old STUPID; it stops all movement and completely blocks all self-love. I would say that it is one of life's hardest yet most important lessons. I wish for you my dear mother that you would dig down deep so you can forgive yourself completely and see what beautiful changes that will bring about for you."*

_ I have to say that I do forgive myself for certain things and things I don't even know about and it feels good for a little while. Then it seems to go away, the good feeling, that is. It makes me feel like I don't do it right or that I have more to forgive myself for. So I am asking you my boy if you can shed some light on this for me.

"I see the frustration in your energy mom. All I can really tell you is that it is better for you to just keep forgiving yourself than it is to keep it inside. Not forgiving is very ugly energy, just keep doing the best you can, and don't be so hard on yourself. Just say this little prayer, make it a habit. Do it every day for a month and see how you feel. I FORGIVE MYSELF COMPLETELY, BECAUSE I LOVE MYSELF THAT MUCH AND I DO! AMEN"

_ Ben is there anything you would like to tell me about your brothers or tell your brothers for you?

"Yes, that they are all so awesome! They really are mom; I know that you are doing the best you can. You need to know you have done and will continue to do a great job. However, they do need to be told more often how awesome you think they are. You cannot tell them that too much."

"They all have strong spiritually based gifts, but they may not want to develop them till much later on in life, like you. They cannot be pushed into using these gifts only supported when they ask for it."

"The oldest one is cool and everything else, besides loving him I really like him too. He has a strange sense of humour, but that is part of what makes him the individual he is. He needs to work on his self-love, but he is still young and he will be able to figure things out. He's an amazing artist and has incredible talent. You worry too much about him and need to trust that you did a better job with him than you think. He is a very intelligent young man, so you do not have to have

any concerns there. I believe he will need some kind of help, maybe a non-judgemental ear somewhere down the road for abandonment issues, because of dad, but not a lot if it is good therapy for him, and he needs to know that it was not his fault when dad left."

"When you feel it is appropriate I would like you to tell him if he feels he is in competition with me that he has me beat hands down on experience alone. Tell him I love him very much and I always have."

"The second one has very strong energy and is the most like me, but you know that. Thank you for not treating him any differently because of that. He could be a comedian with his sense of humour, much different from his older brother. He makes me laugh all the time. He has a lot of stuff in his brain, sometimes it looks too full. Watch him for headaches. He will find his passion sooner than later. He will enjoy what he does and that is huge now a days. You will have to watch him (Just like the other two) with the girls' mom; I believe the saying is LADYKILLER. When you have the chance, please tell him that I love him so much, but he knows that already and is quite conscious of it. He also needs to know often how awesome he is. He too will need some help with his dad. He seems to be pretty connected with his stepdad and that helps him a lot."

"The youngest one, WOW, he is something hey mom? He will develop his Spiritual gifts and use them in what he ends up doing for a living, kind of like you. He has a huge heart and will require some help from you when it comes to direction. He will make a

difference in the world with his compassion for life. I remember how you used to say that I was so full of life, but that kid is so full he overflows, I can see it from here and that is awesome. He does not need a lot of help when it comes to dad, because he has totally adopted his stepdad, but he also has abandonment issues. Some go much deeper than this lifetime for him. He too has an incredible sense of humour and is a very happy young man. You have a long and deep connection with him, again something you already know. He knows how awesome he is, but still needs it to be reinforced due to outside influences and that is because of his personality. You can tell him that I really enjoy hanging out with him, he has great energy and that I know he has seen me a time or two."

_ What about that sister of yours Ben?

"Well, she has been a challenge for you, but you know in your heart that it has all been worth it. This recent obstacle that she has encountered with the break up has been a huge challenge for all of you, but a really big one for her. She will come around pretty soon and get back into a routine, but she still has some more to deal with in that situation. Her self-esteem is the lowest of all my siblings, but that is her life path that she has chosen. Part of what she is going through now is so that she can bond with her stepdad, because that fatherly image is still very important to her. As the only girl she totally needs a loving and supportive relationship with him. She had the longest relationship with dad therefore needs the most help. Mom you need

to tell her of all the good times she had with dad and how much in love they were with each other, I feel that would help her right now."

"Please continue to tell her what a wonderful person she is and how important she is to this family. That will help her tremendously to go forward and be the strong and loving person she is."

"My hope for her is to see that I was a wonderful gift to our family and be grateful for all the extra time she had with me, but right now she feels abandoned by me as well. Tell her again mom that I am with her a lot and we will be doing some channelling work together in the near future as she too has Spiritual gifts."

_ Are there any other Spirits with you that would like to share anything that would benefit the reader or myself?

"First of all, my grandma is here poking me in the ribs, I take it she would like to start."

"My dear daughter and only girl, I want to tell you how much I love you and always have. You have done me proud in the area of motherhood. You did a much better job than I, only because you searched for a better way, found it and applied it to your life. You and I had the same amount of children (Five) and raised the same amount (Four). The fact that my first baby girl was stillborn made me very bitter and that never went away while I was on earth. I am truly sorry for that to all of you. When Benjamin passed I could see your pain and was sending you so much love. *I know you couldn't feel it at the time, but I just kept doing it and felt I had to, as your mother. I was right there to get Benjamin when he passed; I want you to know that."*

"It's wonderful to see how you get along with your two brothers and nice to see the support that you give each other. I want to thank you, since I have this incredible opportunity, for all that you did for your little brother and dad after I passed away. You had to grow up so quickly. I'm sorry for that, but you did a great job."

"My dear girl, you have done and are doing such a fantastic job with your children, they are so beautiful and healthy. I want to reassure you that I have been helping with my granddaughter's healing and recovery. I will not leave my post until she no longer needs me. Even then I will not be far."

"Thank you for breaking the links in the chain that you did, they will make a huge loving, and much needed change for generations. I'm sorry I couldn't do more for you while I was there, but that was all part of the Divine plan as you know."

"Your youngest reminds me of you when you were young, he's a real 'Chatter Box'. He will also turn out most like you and continue to break links, where needed, with so much compassion in his heart...."

"My grandma has now stepped back for grandpa to have a turn."

"I first want to thank you my dearest girl and my sons for allowing me to pass with dignity. Also for you telling me, and knowing I would hear you, that

your mother was waiting to take me home. As soon as I let go, there she was. She was so beautiful it took my breath away, excuse the pun. It was a magnificent reunion, and the vision you had of us dancing was exactly what happened."

"I also thank you for not having any unfinished business or regrets with me. That really made it easier on you and easier on me for the process I had to go through when I first arrived here. It was wonderful to be best friends with my daughter the last ten to twelve years; I know it wasn't that way always, we both had to work on it. The day you were born was one of the very best days of my life. I really did see you as my princess and the most amazing gift."

"I don't mean to toot our own horns, but your mother and I are like the best grandparents we can be from here. I always told you how beautiful your kids were and how well you were doing with them. You should be very pleased with your progress my darling girl."

"One last thing, besides how much I love you, I want to tell you that you are surrounded by guides, Angels and Archangels honey, please know this. You are never, ever alone...."

"Both grandma and grandpa have stepped back for now, but if you could only see the loving energy that they are sending you right now...."

"Mom, I hear thousands of voices right now from children over here calling out all over the world to their loved ones, how much they still and always will love them. There are parents calling to their children and

161

children calling to their parents and siblings how they are still with them always and in all ways. It is quite amazing; they must have seen or sensed the open connection between us. It is like beautiful music, I wish you could hear it."

_ Ben I am just thrilled and so very grateful I asked this question. I had no idea what would come, thank you so much son for being a conduit for this visit. I could not have asked for more today.

Thank you, mom and dad, so much for your kind and loving words and the love that you continue to send to me and our family. If I could see that loving energy I bet it would look like the most beautiful rainbow I could ever imagine. Thank you to all three of you. What a wonderful gift, I feel ever so blessed.

_ Ben, what can you tell us about the elemental realm? (Fairies, wood nymphs, pixies, gnomes and so on.)

"It most definitely does exist. Normally human vibrations are lower, which makes it hard to see these beautiful little creatures. They, like Angels, have a much higher vibration then humans. They are just little Angels. Angels are sent by God to help, care for and guide humans. Elementals are sent by God to look after, care for, and guide animals, plant life and to help with the protection of Mother Earth. Elementals need our help to look after such a big planet and we need to stop hurting Mother Earth and start helping her."

"There is a band, a type of energy I guess you could say, that is wrapped around the planet,

you cannot see it. When humans are born they go through this band. It gives them, let's say, ego. When Angels come to earth they can pass right through it without getting any of that energy on them, but when elementals pass through they like humans get some of this energy on them. This is not bad energy; I would say it is a bit of a misunderstanding of self-love, maybe like a bit of conceit or arrogance. Elements are a bit on the arrogant side. You know that mom that is why you put gazing balls in your fairy gardens so they can admire themselves in the moonlight when no one is looking. I know that you know this, but I am just validating it for you and informing the reader."

"When you want a favour from a fairy, like a healthy garden or something like that, they want you to do something for them first. Maybe they want you to pick up garbage on your walks, make a fairy garden for them or just help mother earth in whatever way you can. So once you have done for them, they have no problem doing for you. They also are asking us to help them with the huge clean-up of our Mother Earth."

"They are busy all the time fixing and making better our planet for us and it is their job. They do rest though and have fun, they love to play at night in and around water, flowers and in the forest, and they are also quite attached to children. Because children have a much higher vibration then adults, they can quite often see them."

"I know that you believe mom and one day you will see them, I promise you. Belief comes first, then trust in yourself, which will heighten your vibration.

As you would say 'keep your eyes peeled.' I would say with that you must also have an open heart and mind."

_ Can you please give me more information about signing the contract for you to pass at the young age of five?

"The fact that I was five years old does not matter, that is only in human time. What does matter is that I was finished with that lifetime and had completed why I came. I cannot tell you what my purpose was; because it is something you will learn and understand here when it will be one hundred percent love based. With human judgment it will not be fully understood."

"What I can tell you is when we were all sitting around coming up with and signing this particular contract, we all had complete and full understanding of why it was going to happen. The man on the bike with me also signed. I was not afraid, you and dad were not sad and my sister and brothers were not mad because all of those are earthly feelings."

"Over here there is nothing but pure love and understanding. There is no experience or the feelings of that here, that is why we go to earth. All eight of us had a full understanding here of this and not until you experienced it there, the pain of losing a loved one, was the contract fulfilled."

"When all of us are here again we will be able to talk about this without any pain at all and we will sign more contracts like that one. It is all for the purpose of each individual's soul growth. We contract

with others in our soul circles for growth. No one soul comes to the earth completely alone, because you need the energy and lessons of others to fulfill your contracts. This doesn't mean you can't have a lonely life it just means you are not alone."

"This is not for payback, it is only about growth, sharing and helping each other's souls. I say that it is not about paybacks, because I felt you thinking of the lifetime I told you about when I was your mother and you were the pirate that did not return home. As I said before, when we are all here again at the contract table we will be able to see all that we have learned and all that we still need to learn in total and complete truth."

_ Does the part of your soul that stays there always have a job and if so what is it?

"Yes I do. I work with young children and babies that have passed by accident or sudden death, just like me. Sometimes when somebody dies by an accident, not by accident, because there is no such thing, do you know what I mean? Accidents happen, but nothing happens by accident. For example my (Accident) was planned out to be exactly what it was, it did not happen by accident at all. Sometimes when people pass suddenly, they die so quickly they do not know what is going on. They sometimes do not know they are dead even when they can see their bodies from above."

"Most times babies and children do not experience that 'not knowing'. It has not been that long since they were here, so they know what is going on.

They also have not had enough time to be humanized, I guess I could say. They are still innocent, so I help them find their Angels and soul circles. Then they can get on with their journey on this side."

"They do not all need me, some are old souls and they know exactly what to do when they leave their bodies. But new or young souls do not know and as their deaths were sudden they can be confused and that is where I come in. Sometimes they stay confused until I can bring them to someone from their soul circle, that is when they will recognize that soul and at the same time who and where they are."

"That is the glorifying part of my job, their recognition of who they really are. That creates a beautiful energy and incredible colors come from the soul when they realize they are HOME. That is like a paycheque when I see and feel that vibration of recognition."

_ Do we have soul names that we are called on the other side?

"Yes, but names are not needed here, like they are on earth. Only the human mind is the one that needs names. On this side you just know who someone is by their energy. See, you know who you really are when you are here and that is what energy you put out."

"What I do know, is when you ask for names of your Angels or guides from us over here you are quite often told "Names are not important," that is because here they are not. All you really need to do is think of that Angel or guide and they will be by your side

instantly. I know you feel very blessed to know the names of your three healing guides, but you know you just have to think of them right?"

"Mom I think it would be a good idea to tell the readers how you got the name of your third healing Angel, don't you?"

_ That's a good idea honey, I will. One evening my husband was giving me a healing and he said that he felt that there were three healing Angels helping him with me besides his Angels. So I asked him to describe them to me. The first two I was already aware of, but it was the third one that was new. He told me that it was a young Tibetan boy about eight or nine years old. I asked him to ask for his name and he told me that the young boy had just walked away and what he was seeing faded at that point. Ever since then when I do a healing and call on my guides I ask for the first two by name and then I call "Just walked away" and he is there by my side, instantly. Now back to you Ben.

"On this side we just feel in our heart centers who we want and that soul, that energy, will appear before us. I understand that as humans it is easier to call on someone, human or Spirit by name, because of the mind. I suppose when you know the name of your guardian Angel it is much easier to just call on them when you feel you need them to help you our just be by your side. I can see how that would be a comfort rather than wondering if they can hear you or

*not. It is very simple, just believe they are with you
and they are."*

**_ I was wondering Ben if you had any advice on how
to make it easier for more people to visualize a real
PEACE ON EARTH?**

*"The answer is and will always be LOVE! Where
does this incredibly strong love come from you may
ask? It comes from the heart, the heart consciousness.
There are only two emotions on the planet, LOVE
and FEAR. When you make all decisions from the
heart they will always be love based, but when you
pull from the human brain there is room for thinking
and thinking can be either love or fear based. I am not
knocking thinking, the human brain has advanced us
so far, but at what cost. It is now time for more and
more humans to live from the heart consciousness;
there is more love that way. The more loving people
you have in the world the better chance we have of
heightening the vibrations. I know I keep telling you
this, but it must happen. It is that important."*

*"It is not that far off; I believe it will happen in
your lifetime mom, the vision of peace on earth will
bring you all, the truth."*

**_ Can you tell me Ben what you think about this book,
your part in it and its purpose?**

*"I am excited about it and I have been since the
very mention of a book. I believe you wrote this book
from a hero's standpoint, not a victim's, and for that
reason I do not think you could have even started it*

until you got over being a victim. I think you did a wonderful and honest job in part one mom. When I gave you the impression that I was going to be your co-author I had no idea yet of this part of the book. I guess it took me about six months, in your time, and then I was moved to tell you about part two. I know you were rather excited about this part, and the beautiful energy that emulated from you told me the truth of the outcome, but when you started THINKING about it and doubting yourself, all that beautiful light stopped coming from your heart. That was very sad, but a wonderful example of the difference between heart-feeling and head-thinking for you, anyway."

"When I first gave you that message I saw it go right to your heart, then your heart felt the outcome of such an idea and you lit right up. By the time it got to your head and you started thinking it was like you turned off the light switch. Then you started thinking about how you could possibly do this and then more on how you could not do this. That was sad for me to see that whole change come about, mind you it was interesting. I learned what low self-confidence can do to someone and how it can happen so quickly and without merit. So, that is why I have been behind you and pushing you so hard. I know when you are busy, but I also know when you are just being stubborn and hard on yourself. That is one of the hardest things to watch from here, even though it may serve a purpose, is when you, my dad or my sister blame yourselves. I have a really hard time watching that, but I do see a brighter future for all of you and that makes it easier

169

for me. I know it is kind of cheating on my part, but that is okay. That is one of the privileges I have from here."

"Anyways mom, I really believe your experiences in this book and those of the rest of the family will help a lot of people. So I have put in for a special blessing from this side to do just that."

_ Is it true that when people pass away, that some souls choose to not go directly into the light and if so, why?

"Deep rooted fear! There are a few different reasons why a soul would avoid the light after they pass. Anyone who has been brought up with the 'WRATH OF GOD' or the 'DAMNATION' could and most likely will have issues at this point. This is so old and out dated, however there still are people on the planet that believe God will judge them and then they will PAY.... 'THE JUDGEMENT DAY!' You are your own judge; I think God would be a lot easier on most people then themselves when it comes to judging. I spoke to God personally about this one and was told "There is NO purpose in me judging perfection, for I will always and forever see it as that and you all will too, but only from here." Sometimes people are so afraid of penance and punishment that they may see a flicker of light after they pass and think it is flames and damnation, then hightail it out of there."

"Another reason is new souls that need a lot of guidance. They can get lost, but not for long before help comes from their higher selves, their guides and

workers like me. Older souls, not older people per se, know when they pass away exactly what to do. They get over here in record time and do not need any help. Mom I believe that is why a soul that has passed would benefit from your prayers. You want to pray for them to go straight home with no detours or delays. Once the soul lets go of the mind all of this changes."

"When you first pass, your soul leaves your earthly vehicle, your body, but does not get rid of the mind right away. That is why if you believe in hell, judgement and damnation that is what you will experience, but only until you are able to leave the mind behind as well. This is where our soul memory comes in, which is not of the mind. On the other hand if you believe in beautiful Angels, love and rainbows just like me, that is what your mind will bring to you and you will experience. I hope I answered that enough for you. It really is a perfect world and all will happen as it should."

_ Why would someone that has had a really hard life on earth, ever want to come back here to what might just be more of the same thing?

"Well, that is a good question. What one sees as a hard life is a perception of that persons thinking mind. When you pass over in a short time you will lose that thinking part, but not that of the soul memory."

"When you are here there are stages to go through from arrival to departure into a new life. During one of the first stages you will learn all that you did on earth and other places, whether it was

right, wrong or indifferent, with the help of your soul circle and Guides for understanding. Then when you are ready you will go on to the next stage where you will discuss what is needed in your next lifetime, then sign the contracts for that and then on to the next stage."

"So to answer your question I would say they would not do it again, not exactly the same way. Let's put it this way mom, would you sign up to lose another child next time with what you have gone through and what you know? No! Of course not, but once you get here and have the unconditional love and understanding of the growth and purpose you may very well sign up again. If it is to serve your highest and best good or to help someone else in your circle to grow, you would. The only way you can change this on the earth and in that lifetime is to change the way you see it. You know that phrase "If you change the way you look at things the things you look at change." That is so true, they have to change, it is a universal law, however sometimes the way we change things is not for our highest good and things can seem worse. I believe the more you learn about who you really are the better choices you will make in each lifetime."

_ Why do some people struggle with addictions where others do not at all?

"Addiction is a very hard earthly lesson to learn and some may need to struggle with it in different ways and in many lifetimes. If a lesson is not learned

completely, it will be brought back to you again and again until it is fully learned. And you are the one, your higher self that keeps bringing it back to you."

"It's not about your personality or your will power as opposed to another's, it is just what you need to do if that is what you have chosen and only you can do it."

"There is good news though, for those of you out there that struggle with addiction in this lifetime, once you have won the battle against your addictions you will not have to deal with that addiction again in another lifetime. You may have to experience some of it to help others next time, but it will never be as hard again."

"The hardest thing to do when you have addictions is to love yourself anyways; it is the hardest and the most important thing to do. Love and forgive yourself! All of this is about growth for your soul's journey and is for your highest and best good."

"I feel from here that the people on the planet are slowly starting to get what it is all about. I believe there is so much addiction, because people do not love themselves. The people that raised them did not love themselves either and so on. What I am seeing now is that people are starting to see that and they are teaching the children, theirs and others, what beautiful and lovable people they are and this in time will change the world. One day the addict population will go way down when the self-love goes way up, but as the saying goes Rome was not built in a day!"

"I wish to all addicts that they could, if only for a moment, see their real and beautiful truth reflected in

the mirror, but they must look deeply into their own
eyes. Then healing can begin."

**_ I had explained earlier that my husband and I were
going to do some trance work with Ben if it was ok, and
here are the results. I will keep all that I say in bold and
put what my husband says and what comes through him
in italics. He is now in a deep trance, he has asked and
received permission from Ben, and we have begun.**

**Okay are you feeling any presence there at all, or
coming?**

> *"Yes, I'm feeling some energy, but it's not Ben.*
> *The energy is a little stand-offish. I feel that something*
> *has not been approved of, some kind of permission like*
> *I am not supposed to be here."*

**Okay then, I would like you to ask of your higher
self if it's alright for you to participate in this.**

> *"I have asked and I get a yes, but the energy has*
> *not changed. It's not bad energy, but it seems to have*
> *a feeling of protection to it, I don't understand."*

**I believe that you have to ask my higher self if it's
ok that you act as a conduit to bring Ben forward. Can
do you do that please?**

> *"Yes. I get a yes, and right away I feel a very*
> *strong energy here. The other energy is still here, but*
> *has stepped back a bit. I can't see anything it just*
> *seems very misty. There is a young man here that*

loves kids. He looks after kids when they have passed away, helping to direct children from sudden death, to their loved ones and Angels, because they can get confused.

I have asked, and a couple of questions have been approved."

I now ask my husband's first question of the two questions that he wrote down before I put him in a trance.

_ As far as understanding and hearing people that have crossed over, is there a quicker way to communicate with them like meditation or channelling?

"There is no quicker way. If you understand, meditate, and meditate often you will have more of an opportunity. When you are in a meditative state it is easier to pick up on feelings and sense things. There are other ways to do this, but they must all be love based. I guess you could say that it would be quicker if it comes from the heart then the head. Everyone has a gift to connect, but you have to learn what way works for you. I had this gift since I was born and I think my mom knew it, but she did not know of hers yet. People will push it back if they do not use it, which is why when you get older you do not think you can do it, but you can."

My husband went silent, meaning he's done with that answer.

175

_ The next question is: How can we get the elemental world to help us help them, so they can be a support bridge for the Spirit world?

"This is much like the first question in that you must have an open heart and some kind of an understanding that they are real. You need to connect with them and be close to them. They are very wise and knowledgeable, but shy. They will not come to you; you must go searching for them to create a relationship with them."

Silences again, so I wondered if I could ask another question since my husband still seemed to be quite comfortable in his trance state. I know this is a repeated question, but I wondered what the answer would be, asking it differently. So here it goes: Ben, what do you think about this book?

"Honoured, this book will help my brothers understand a bit about why I am here and why I was there. I want to tell you that a contract is a contract no matter the outcome."

"Do not push the book mom; allow what is to happen just to happen. That is all."

I wanted to ask about the other energy that was with Ben, so I asked if it was my mother, but I got a no. My husband said it feels like male energy. Then I asked if it was my dad and I got a yes. So I asked my dad if he had anything he wanted to say.

"The book my dear will be published when it is published. You worry too much about things and I see your lack of joy, but it's there I can see that too. Bring it out; it's safe to do so. I'm sending you a lot of love, and by for now."

Husband is speaking now. *"Did your dad have a real hardy laugh? I'm asking, because he and Ben are giving me an impression that they are together a lot and laugh all the time. The energies seem to be fading away now."*

*"Oh, Ben is running back and saying, "What do **you** think of the book mom?" He is fading again, but I think you should answer him."*

Well, thanks for asking Ben. I think it has been wonderful therapy for me and very healing. Now that you have said it, I'm hoping it will help your brothers and sister understand more, I hadn't thought of that. It has been a hard book to write, but I hope it can help others. I'm so grateful for the opportunity to spend so much time with you Ben, thank you.

"Both energies are going away now, but they are showing me something funny, they are stuck together like magnets."

I gently took my husband out of the trance state and told him all that happened when he was under, because he gets total amnesia which can be quite common. He is amazed at the whole communication and is quite happy that he was able to do that for us.

_ *This is not a question, it's a statement of my gratitude for my son and all that he has done for me in this book and bringing me the messages from my parents. It is like a love letter to my boy.*

To my dearest Benjamin and very favourite Angel,

I don't know where to begin. I am ever so grateful for the time that you have put into this book with me. Guiding me on and at times giving that push from behind that I needed. I know that time is no never mind to you, but in earthly hours you did put in a lot for me.

I was very grateful for the message that your grandpa, my dad, is with you a lot, because you did have a strong connection with him when you were both here. A huge thank you, Ben for bringing both my parents to talk to me. That was a special and unexpected treat for me and proves to me how strong an unbreakable bond is.

You were such a sweet boy Benjamin when you were here on earth. You had incredible charisma and you were bursting at the seams with a love for life. Maybe it was because you were putting a whole lifetime into just five "Little" years.

Ever since you passed I have always known that you were not far away from me. That was not just a feeling, it was actually a knowing. I thank you for picking me to be your mother in this lifetime.

Thank you for playing your part with me and most of all thank you for loving us so much that you stepped up to sign that contract for all of us. You are my brave little Angel. You have been responsible for teaching me so much, enough for another book I would say.

There just aren't enough words in the English language to express the love and gratitude that I have for you Ben, but I am sure that you can see it coming from my heart to yours. I want to let you know if by chance you have another book that you need to write, I would love to do this again and again with you even if it's just for us. I don't want this to end, but I trust that we have opened up a very special line of communication with each other.

Love always & Forever, your mom.

_ Ben, is there any last words of wisdom from you before I end this book?

"You have done a great job mom with all of this and you are not done yet, by all means. I know there is lots of work you have left to do before this book is on the shelves all over the world, but just because we are not going to communicate on a regular base any more, please know that I am always just as close to you as I am right now! And isn't that the point to this book anyway?"

"I have to say that I have enjoyed doing this book with you, mom, I did have to push you at times, but we made it!'

"You have an incredible future ahead of you mom and I am not saying any more than that because I do not want to wreck any surprises for you. You do need and will learn some more patience and a lot more faith and believe in whom you really are and it is coming. Stop all the worry (You really are not that bad and

have come a very long way.) about my sister and brothers as you know you cannot do anything about the paths that they have chosen. Continue to give them unconditional love, support and accept them for who they are."

"I will tell you this, all your children will end up doing what they are passionate about and it will not take them a lifetime, just continue to encourage them with your love and know that they all love you forever AND FOR ALWAYS."

"Just a quick note on my dad, I know you have some concerns there, but you need not. As with you mom, dad is following the exact path that he lay out for himself in this lifetime. When you two are here on this side discussing your lives, all will be understood and love based, I can guaranty that."

"Your new husband will lovingly stick by your side and all of his step children and grandchildren to come mom and all will be exactly as it should. I know you are getting tired of me saying that, but I know that you learn by repetition, so there."

"I love you immensely mom and this has been a pleasure and believe it or not a wonderful learning experience for me as well and I even had fun. Last bit of advice for you mom is: PLEASE LET YOUR LIGHT SHINE EVER SO BRIGHTLY, BECAUSE THAT IS WHO YOU REALLY ARE!!!"

_ Note to the readers from Benjamin....

"I hope and wish that my mom and I were able to touch you in your heart. I am so sorry to those of you that have had to go through the experience of losing a child this time. I want you to know they are not gone, they are not dead, because there is NO such thing, and they are much closer than you think. There are so many young ones that I have helped to pass from your world to the Spirit world that, ask me "How can I let my parents and siblings know how much I still love them?" So to all of you that will listen with your hearts hear this;

"I LOVE YOU SO MUCH, FOREVER AND FOR ALWAYS!"

"I hope that my experience through my mom can help others understand better, even if we only touch a few hearts we have done better than not touching any."

"I have watched, my mom, dad and siblings throughout the years and they really are doing the best they can and they will continue to do so. I wish the same to all of you."

"If you know anyone that this book could help, please, please do not hesitate to share it with them and pass it along."

"I can say this: To all of you that have lost a child, they have not and will not ever stop loving you, no matter what! This I can promise you!"

"Remember, we are all one living in the heart of God, and God is living in the hearts of all of us, there really is no separation."

"This is not the end; it is the beginning of your understanding. . . ."

CPSIA information can be obtained at www.ICGtesting.com
Printed in the USA
LVOW05s0107180713

343377LV00001B/4/P